A Simple Guide
to
Python GUI
using
the
Standard Tkinter Library

(Windows / Mac / Linux)

AE Johnson

Cover by author.

Contents

Introduction

About the Author

I've been working in IT related roles for nearly 40 years. Despite that, I've never really been a software developer. I started to dabble in programming in my early teens, writing BASIC programs on a Compukit UK101. At school I learned CESIL, more BASIC and a little about other languages such as COBOL and FORTRAN. When I first started work I used COBOL, SCOBOL and TACL (yes, I know) before quickly deciding that I didn't want to spend my life looking at a green (or amber) monitor and moved into data networking where I learned about Routing and Switching, LAN and WAN, Wi-Fi and TCP/IP primarily using the products of Cisco Systems before specialising in Unified Communications. It has been much later in life that I have done a little programming again and I've been delighted to learn Python.

Why Python?

I program in Python primarily due to its simplicity, ease of use, vast collection of libraries and modules and cross-platform compatibility. The language has a readable syntax, making it a great choice for both beginners and experienced programmers. Python allows the user to focus on solving problems without worrying about low-level implementation details, making it a productive and efficient choice for a variety of tasks.

Why Tkinter?

I quickly learned to create useful (but ugly) programs in Python but as I work mainly in Windows, really wanted to add a GUI. Like many other people, I like my programs to have a good looking and intuitive user interface. I soon learned that Tkinter was the de facto standard for GUI development with Python as it is included as a standard library.

A few acronyms

GUI = Graphical User Interface

TCL = Tool Command Language

Tk = A GUI Library developed for TCL

Tkinter = The Python interface for Tk

Ttk = Themed Tkinter

What this book is and what it isn't

This book is intended to be a quick start for people creating a GUI for Python using Tkinter. The idea is to explain using many examples that the reader can adapt and experiment with. I own a small collection of Python books and have also taken (or at least started) a numbers of on-line Python courses. There is the rub. I usually persist with any learning until the point where I have either learned enough to fulfil my immediate need or I have got bored or the subject has become too complex. This is exactly what happened with Python, I managed to write functional code to accomplish what I wanted but wanted to add a 'normal' windows style interface to make my code easier to use and more accessible for non-technical users.

What is Tkinter? Tkinter is a standard Python library for creating graphical user interfaces (GUIs) that run on the desktop. It provides a set of tools and widgets that can be used to build graphical interfaces, including buttons, labels, text boxes, and other standard GUI elements. A Tkinter widget is a graphical element in the GUI (Graphical User Interface) of a Python application that can be used to display various types of information or to receive user input. Examples of Tkinter widgets include buttons, labels, text boxes, and drop-down menus.

This is very much designed to be a 'getting started' type book so I'm not going to include alternative options, lots of historical background or too much detail on the more advanced options or troubleshooting. This book is not designed to be a complete Tkinter reference – it's more about learning from simple examples and encouraging the reader to get stuck in, to experiment and to explore further.

If you get stuck, I would recommend looking at the documentation at http://tkdocs.com/ or at some of the great web sites such as *stackoverflow.com*

Why use Tkinter

Tkinter is easy to use and comes bundled with most Python installations, making it a popular choice for building simple desktop applications. One of the great things about Tkinter is that your program will most likely run on Windows, Mac and Linux with either very little or no modification. In this book, I'll use Windows for the examples.

Tkinter is the most widely used and commonly known GUI library for Python, as it comes bundled with the standard Python distribution. However, there are several other popular GUI libraries for Python that are used for specific purposes or offer alternative features, such as:

- PyQt: A set of Python bindings for the Qt application framework and runs on all platforms supported by Qt including Windows, OS X, Linux, iOS, and Android.
- wxPython: A set of Python bindings for the wxWidgets C++ library, which provides native look-and-feel on a number of different platforms.
- Kivy: An open-source, cross-platform Python library for developing mobile apps and other multitouch application software with a natural user interface.

Ultimately, the choice of which GUI library to use depends on the specific requirements of your project and your personal preferences. This book will focus solely on Tkinter.

Start here - jump straight in!

As I'm writing this it is 2024 and I'm going to assume that you are using Python 3. All my examples have been tested with Python 3 on a PC running Windows11.

I'm not going to cover Tkinter installation here as it comes bundled with the standard Python distribution. From the command prompt you can check that Tkinter is installed and which version that you have in case you need to troubleshoot:

```
PS C:\Users\> python
Python 3.12.2 (tags/v3.12.2:6abddd9, Feb  6 2024, 21:26:36) [MSC v.1937 64 bit (AMD64)] on win32
Type "help", "copyright", "credits" or "license" for more information.
>>> import tkinter
>>> tkinter._test()
```

The **tkinter._test()** command will launch a small Window like this:

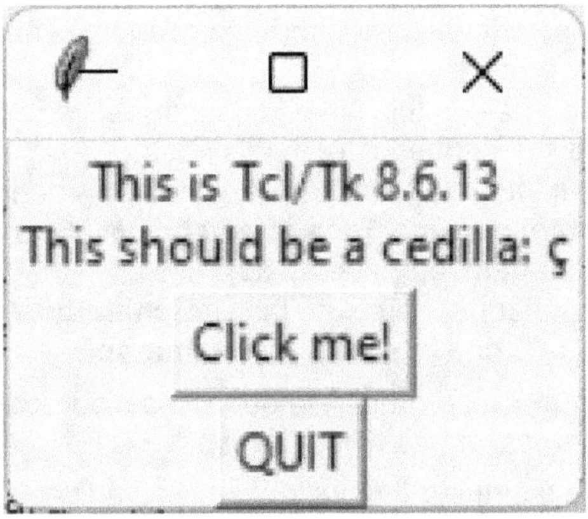

Which should act to reassure you that all is working.

Hello World!

Lets get started with the traditional “Hello World!” program.

```
import tkinter as tk

root = tk.Tk()
root.title("Hello World!")

label = tk.Label(root, text="Hello World!")
label.pack()

root.mainloop()
```

Output:

Most Python/Tkinter programs will follow this basic layout:

- import libraries – in this case just tkinter with **import tkinter as tk**
- **from tkinter import ttk** – if you are going to use the ttk themed Tkinter widgets – more on this later
- setup the window (called root here, you can use something else like window if you prefer)
- define our widgets – in this case just the **label** widget. There are many Tkinter widgets described later in this book.
- define how our widgets will fit into the window – done here using the **pack()** geometry manager (one of several options available see Tkinter Geometry Managers later in the book)
- initiate our mainloop – here with the **root.mainloop()** command. There should always be one and only one **mainloop().**

In this example, the root or main Window is called root which seems to be traditional although you can call it what you like.

After defining this, the first thing that we do is give it a title. It may be that when you run this, the Window is too small to view the title but for the moment you can expand it manually to check that it has worked. You can change the title later if you wish.

The next thing that I have done is to define a label widget for the root window and assign it the text “Hello World!”. I could also have put the text on a button or used the more versatile text widget but more on that later.

The next thing **label.pack()** which 'packs' the label widget into the window. The pack method of geometry management is one of three options mentioned in this book. It is the easiest to use and is therefore used in many of the examples. For a real-world project, I prefer the grid method (see the section on Geometry Management below) which provides much more control but for now, pack is easy and will work fine.

The final line here is **root.mainloop()** which effectively created the window as defined and starts an infinite loop which monitors the widgets for activity until such time as the window is closed with a **root.destroy()**

How to Import Tkinter

Both **import tkinter as tk** and **from tkinter import** * are valid ways to import the **tkinter** module in Python. However, there are some differences between these two methods that you should be aware of.

import tkinter as tk imports the **tkinter** module and assigns it an alias (**tk** in this case). This means that you can access the functions, classes, and variables defined in the **tkinter** module by using the **tk** prefix. For example:

import tkinter as tk root = tk.Tk()

label = tk.Label(root, text="Hello, World!")

In this case, the **Tk()** function and **Label()** class are both accessed using the **tk** prefix.

from tkinter import * imports all the public names (functions, classes, and variables) defined in the **tkinter** module directly into your namespace. This means that you can use the names without any prefix. For example:

from tkinter import *

root = Tk() label = Label(root, text="Hello, World!")

In this case, the **Tk()** function and **Label()** class can be used directly without the **tk.** prefix.

However, using **import tkinter as tk** is generally considered to be a better practice than using **from tkinter import** *. This is because the latter method can cause naming conflicts if you accidentally import names that conflict with names you have defined in your own code. It can also make it harder to read and understand your code if you're not sure where a particular name came from. Therefore, it's usually a better idea to use **import tkinter as tk** and then prefix the names from the **tkinter** module with **tk.** to make it clear where they come from.

The Lifecycle of a Python/Tkinter App

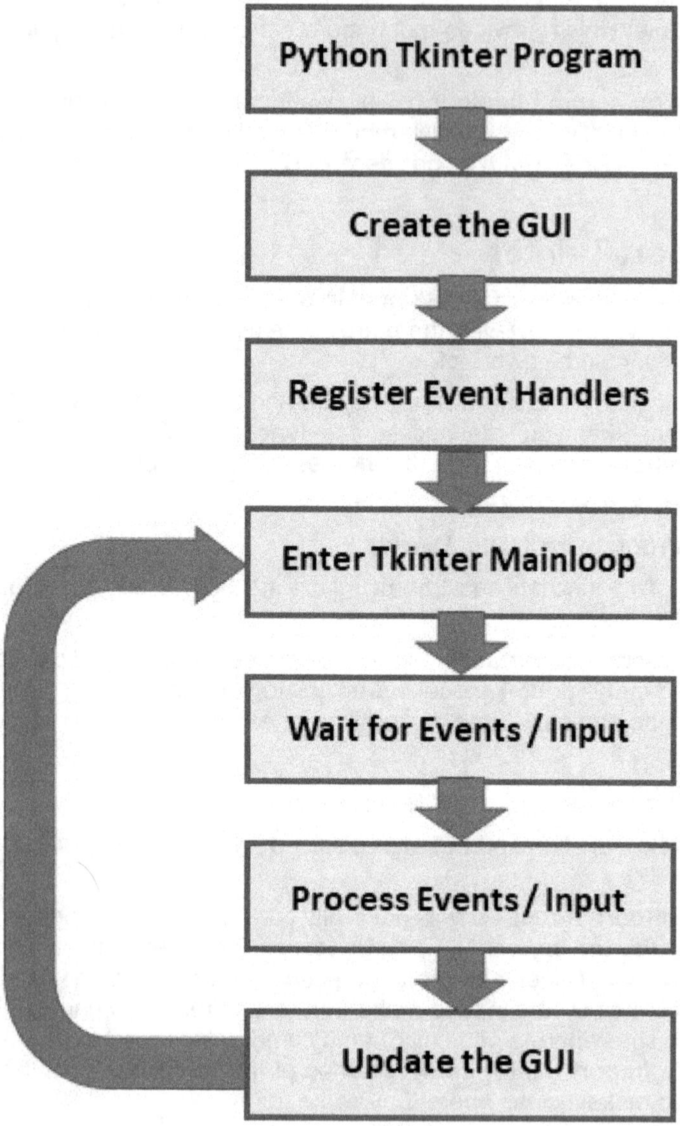

1. The Python Tkinter program starts by creating the graphical user interface (GUI) of the application.
2. Next, event handlers are registered for various components of the GUI. These event handlers are functions that are executed when a particular event, such as a button click, occurs.
3. The program enters the Tkinter mainloop, which is an infinite loop that waits for events and input from the user.

4. When an event or input is received, the program processes it using the appropriate event handler.
5. After the event has been processed, the program updates the display of the GUI to reflect any changes that were made.
6. The program then returns to the Tkinter mainloop to wait for the next event or input.

This process repeats until the user closes the application.

Creating Windows

Once you have defined your window using the appropriate widgets and your chosen geometry manager the **mainloop()** command e.g. **window.mainloop()** or **root.mainloop()** will create the window until such time as it is destroyed.

Here we have the same code as in my first example but I've replaced **root** with **window** and the other text to make it a little more readable. Use whichever you prefer.

```
import tkinter as tk

window = tk.Tk()
window.title("Window Title Goes Here")

label = tk.Label(window, text="Label Text Goes Here")
label.pack()

window.mainloop()
```

Example output (the Window title is there but can't be seen without re-sizing the Window as space is taken up with the controls)

Sizing a window

As you can see from the earlier examples, by default, the window will only be as large as it needs to be. If we change this by using window.geometry (or root.geometry if you have called your window root) so adding **window.geometry("300x100")** you can see that the window is now 300 pixels wide by 100 pixels high. Please note that you need to make sure to use an x and not a * (asterisk or multiplication symbol).

```
import tkinter as tk

window = tk.Tk()
window.title("Window Title Goes Here")
window.geometry("300x100")

label = tk.Label(window, text="Label Text Goes Here")
label.pack()

window.mainloop()
```

As you can see, the whilst the output has the same content as in the previous example, the window dimensions have changed as specified.

Output:

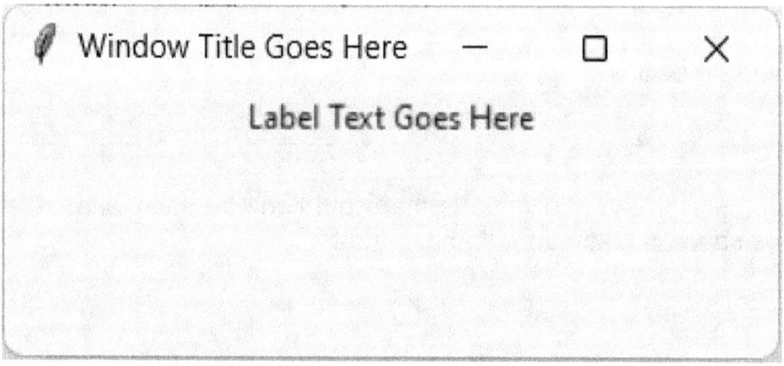

If you want to restrict to what extent the window may be resized you can use minsize and maxsize parameters e.g.:

window.minsize(200,100)

window.maxsize(500,500)

Changing the initial window position

If you want to change the initial location of the window then you can specify an offset as well as the dimensions:

window.geometry("300x100+100+200")

please note to use the lowercase character x not a * (multiplication symbol) and do not leave any spaces between the characters or you will get a **bad geometry specifier** error.

Centring a Window

If you want to create window that is centred on the screen, then there are a number of options but you can do something like this:

```
import tkinter as tk
import tkinter.ttk as ttk

root = tk.Tk()
w = 200 # Window Width
h = 50 # Window Height

scrn_width = root.winfo_screenwidth()  # Width of the screen
scrn_height = root.winfo_screenheight() # Height of the screen

# Calculate Starting X and Y coordinates for Window
x = (scrn_width/2) - (w/2)
y = (scrn_height/2) - (h/2)

root.geometry('%dx%d+%d+%d' % (w, h, x, y))

label = ttk.Label(root, text="Screen width ="+str(scrn_width))
label.pack()
label = ttk.Label(root, text="Screen height ="+str(scrn_height))
label.pack()

root.mainloop()
```

Output:

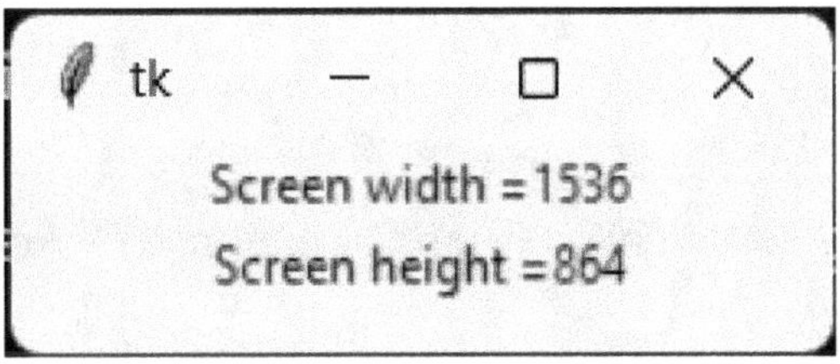

Changing the window icon

If you want to change the little icon in the top left corner, you can change it from the default with a command like:

window.iconbitmap(True, "iconfile.ico")

The "True" option allows this icon to be inherited by child windows.

or

root.iconbitmap(True, r"c:\path\icon.ico")

in this second example the file path is included and the r stands for "raw" and will cause backslashes in the string to be interpreted as actual backslashes rather than special characters as would otherwise be the case with Python.

The .ico file format

All icons for executable files in Windows are saved in the ICO format. Windows ICO files typically store images ranging from 16x16 to 256x256 pixels. Older ICO files only include images up to 48x48 (the dimensions Windows previously recommended). However, most newer icons store images up to 256x256 pixels.

There are a number of free options available online to create ICO files from other picture formats.

Here's a simple example where pressing the button changes the icon:

```
import tkinter as tk

root = tk.Tk()
root.geometry("200x50")

# The "True" option means icon is inherited
root.iconbitmap(True, r"c:\pythonvenv\colour1.ico")

current_icon=1

# Define a function to be called when the button is clicked
def button_clicked():
    global current_icon
    if current_icon == 1:
        root.iconbitmap(True, r"c:\pythonvenv\colour1.ico")
        current_icon = 2
    else:
        root.iconbitmap(True, r"c:\pythonvenv\colour2.ico")
```

```
        current_icon = 1

button = tk.Button(root, text="Click Me", font=("Arial", 14), bg="blue", fg="white", command=button_clicked)
button.pack(padx=10, pady=10)

root.mainloop()
```

Output (the colourful icon top left alternates when the button is clicked):

Closing a Window

There are a couple of ways to exit the mainloop()

You can use **root.quit()** or **root.destroy()**

root.quit() causes mainloop to exit. The interpreter and all the widgets are still intact. If you call this function, you can have code that executes after the call to **root.mainloop()** and that code can interact with the widgets (for example to get a value from an entry widget).

root.destroy() will destroy all the widgets and exit mainloop. Any code after the call to **root.mainloop()** will run, but any attempt to access any widgets (for example, get a value from an entry widget) will fail because the widget no longer exists.

Subwindows

We can create subwindows or child windows with the **Toplevel** command so if we already have a main window called root we can create a child window with **childwin=Toplevel(root)** and then add widgets to it independently from the main window.

In the following example, we create both a main/root window and a child/sub window where each is identified with a label and each has a Quit button. You will notice that the button on the subwindow closes only that window whereas the quit button on the main screen will close both the main and the subwindow.

Example:

```
from tkinter import *
from tkinter import ttk

root = Tk()
```

```
root.geometry("300x150")
root.title("Main Window")

sub_win = Toplevel(root)
sub_win.geometry("300x150+300+300")
sub_win.title("SubWindow")

label_main = Label(root, text="This is the Main Window", font=('Helvetica
15'))
label_main.pack(pady=20)
button_main = Button(root, text="Press to Quit", command=root.destroy)
button_main.pack()

label_sub = Label(sub_win, text="This is a sub Window", font=('Helvetica
15'))
label_sub.pack()
button_sub = Button(sub_win, text="Press to Quit",
command=sub_win.destroy)
button_sub.pack()

root.mainloop()
```

Output:

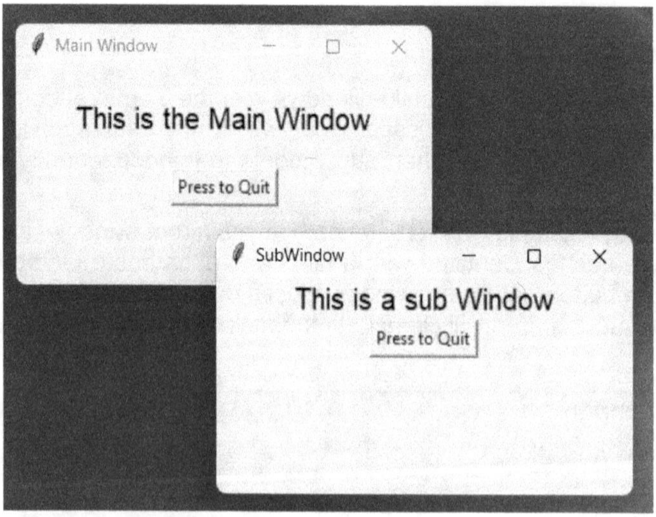

Tkinter and Themed Tkinter ttk

So what is the difference between Tkinter and Themed Tkinter and which should you use? (the answer is probably both), When Tkinter was first introduced in the late 1980s/early 1990s it had only the standard Widgets (about a dozen). In 2009, Themed Tkinter was introduced along with styles.

Standard Tkinter widgets are easy both to use and to customise without having to delve into styles and themes. Themed Tkinter (ttk) has the benefit of bringing six new widgets and also the concept of styles and themes.

Styles control how widgets (like buttons for example) look. They also make for cleaner code and less repetition. If you have many button widgets in your application, rather than having to repeat the exact appearance details every time you create a new one you can instead assign them a style. For more detailed information on Tkinter styles, see the chapter on Styles below.

To start using Themed Tkinter, import its module:

```
from tkinter import ttk
```

To override the basic Tk widgets, the import should follow the Tk import:

```
from tkinter import *
from tkinter.ttk import *
```

What this does is to make several of the tkinter.ttk widgets to replace the standard Tk widgets. The following Widgets are available as both standard and ttk themed widgets:

- Button
- Checkbutton
- Entry
- Frame
- Label
- LabelFrame
- Menubutton
- PanedWindow
- Radiobutton
- Scale

- Scrollbar

There are a number of Widgets available in Themed Tkinter that have no standard equivalent:

- Combobox
- Notebook
- Progressbar
- Separator
- Sizegrip
- Treeview

There are also some standard widgets that have no Themed Tkinter equivalent (this is because in these two cases, the widget itself does not have much visible style) :

- Canvas
- Text

All of these widgets are described in more detail later in the book.

Ttk Tkinter Themes Library

One of the benefits of Themed Tkinter is the ability to create themes. Each Theme is a collection of widget styles. While a style controls the appearance of one class of widget, a theme will control the appearance of the whole user interface.

There are a number of available themes which can be installed and there are many others available online or you can make your own.

If you want to try some existing themes, a good first step is to install the ttkthemes library using pip (the name is a recursive acronym for "Pip Installs Packages")

```
pip install ttkthemes

or if you are not using Windows you may need

pip3 install ttkthemes
```

You can then check from within Python to see which themes you have available:

```
from tkinter import *
from tkinter import ttk

root = Tk()

style = ttk.Style(root)
```

```
style.theme_names()

current_theme = style.theme_use()
```

If you want to check the output, you could create a little piece of code like this which also demonstrates a couple of ttk styles:

```
from tkinter import *
from tkinter import ttk

root = Tk()

style = ttk.Style(root)

style.configure("Blue.TLabel", foreground="blue", background="white",
font= ('Helvetica', '18', 'bold'))
style.configure("Black.TLabel", foreground="black", background="white",
font= ('Times', '18', 'bold'))

txt1 = style.theme_names()
txt2 = current_theme = style.theme_use()

lab = ttk.Label(root, text='Available Themes: ', style="Blue.TLabel")
lab.pack()
lab = ttk.Label(root, text=style.theme_names(), style="Black.TLabel")
lab.pack()
lab = ttk.Label(root, text='Current Theme: ', style="Blue.TLabel")
lab.pack()
lab = ttk.Label(root, text=style.theme_use(), style="Black.TLabel")
lab.pack()

root.mainloop()
```

Output:

Please note that the actual available themes will be different with each Operating System. For example:

Theme	Windows	Mac	Linux
alt	✓	✓	✓
clam	✓	✓	✓
classic	✓	✓	✓
default	✓	✓	✓
vista	✓	×	×
winnative	✓	×	×
xpnative	✓	×	×
aqua	×	✓	×

There is a good list of additional ttk themes available here:

https://wiki.tcl-lang.org/page/List+of+ttk+Themes

Switching Themes

The **style.theme_use()** command can be used to make the selected style active. For example:

```
style = ttk.Style()
style.theme_use("clam")
```

The next example is maybe not the best example of code but does illustrate how the tkinter theme in use can be changed live at the click of a button:

```
from tkinter import *
from tkinter import ttk

root = tk.Tk()
root.geometry("350x250+200+200")

style=ttk.Style()
style.theme_use("default")
style.configure("mybutton.TButton", foreground="blue", font="Verdana
24")

style_num=0
style_names=list(style.theme_names()) # splits the string of style names
into a list

def scale_changed(val):
    font_size = int(val)
```

```
    label.config(font=("TkDefaultFont", font_size))
    progress.config(value=font_size)

def style_changed():
    global style_num, style_names
    style_num += 1
    if style_num == len(style_names): # if num of styles in list reached go back to the first
        style_num = 0
    style.theme_use(style_names[style_num]) # select the style to use from the list
    label.config(text=style.theme_use())

button = ttk.Button(root, text="Push Me!", command=style_changed)
button.pack(padx=10, pady=20)

progress = ttk.Progressbar(root, orient="horizontal", length=200, mode="determinate", value=1, maximum=48)
progress.pack()

scale = tk.Scale(root, from_=1, to=48, orient="horizontal", command=scale_changed)
scale.pack()

label = ttk.Label(root, text=style.theme_use())
label.pack()

root.mainloop()
```

Output:

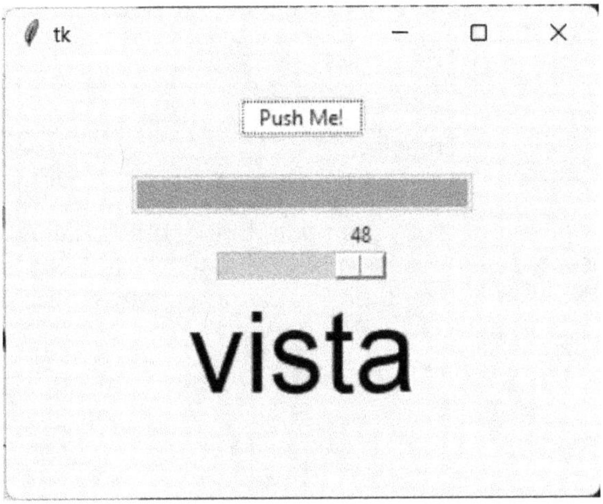

Themed Tkinter Styles

A Style determines the appearance of a ttk widget (not a standard widget). All widgets created with a style will have the same appearance. Each ttk widget has a default style name (see table below) so for a ttk Button widget the default style is TButton.

ttk Widget	Widget Class - Default Style name
Button	TButton
Checkbutton	TCheckbutton
Combobox	TCombobox
Entry	TEntry
Frame	TFrame
Label	TLabel
LabelFrame	TLabelFrame
Menubutton	TMenubutton
Notebook	TNotebook
PanedWindow	TPanedwindow
Progressbar*	Horizontal.TProgressbar or Vertical.TProgressbar, depending on the orient option.
Radiobutton	TRadiobutton
Scale*	Horizontal.TScale or Vertical.TScale, depending on the orient option.
Scrollbar*	Horizontal.TScrollbar or Vertical.TScrollbar, depending on the orient option
Separator	TSeparator
Sizegrip	TSizegrip
Treeview*	Treeview

Each style is composed of many elements that can be customised to create new styles. While it is possible to customise the default styles, it is good practise to customise a style which is based on the default rather than changing the default itself.

Example:

```
# Create a themed style object
style = ttk.Style()

# Define a new style called "Custom.TButton"
style.configure("Custom.TButton", foreground="blue", font=("Arial",
14))

# Create a button widget using the custom style
button = ttk.Button(root, text="Click me", style="Custom.TButton")
```

Tkinter Colours

One of the options that you will most often want to change in the Tkinter widgets is their colour, In Tkinter, there are several ways to represent colours, depending on the context in which the colour is being used.

The most common methods to select a colour:

- **Named colours** Tkinter provides a set of 140 predefined colour names that you can use to specify a colour. For example, you can use "red", "blue", “green” or "yellow" to set the foreground or background colour of a widget.

- **Hexadecimal values** You can also represent colours using a hexadecimal value, which is a six-digit code that represents the amount of red, green, and blue in the colour. The format of the code is **#RRGGBB**, where **RR** is the amount of red, **GG** is the amount of green, and **BB** is the amount of blue, each expressed as a two-digit hexadecimal number. For example, #FF0000 represents pure red, while #00FF00 represents pure green.

- **RGB values** You can also represent colours using an RGB (red-green-blue) tuple, which is a three-tuple that contains the amount of red, green, and blue in the colour, each expressed as an integer between 0 and 255. For example, (255, 0, 0) represents pure red, while (0, 255, 0) represents pure green.

- **RGBA values** Similarly to RGB values, you can represent colours with an RGBA (red-green-blue-alpha) tuple which includes an additional alpha value between 0 and 1 indicating the opacity of the colour. For example, (255, 0, 0, 0.5) represents a semi-transparent red.

Tkinter Styles – a simple example

While it is possible to configure the default styles, It is good practice not to change the default styles, instead create new styles based on the defaults This example configures a style called **mybutton.TButton** (it is based on the default TButton style).

In the code below, It has two changes from the default:

- Blue foreground text
- 24pt Verdana font used

Once you have created a style, you can use it to create as many widgets as you need with the same style.

```
import tkinter as tk
import tkinter.ttk as ttk

class Window:
	def __init__(self, master):
		frame=ttk.Frame(master)
		style=ttk.Style()
		style.configure("mybutton.TButton", foreground="blue",
font="Verdana 24")
		button=ttk.Button(frame, text="Push Me!",
style="mybutton.TButton")
		button.pack(padx=10, pady=20)
		frame.pack(padx=10, pady=10)

root=tk.Tk()
root.geometry("250x150+200+100")
window=Window(root)
root.mainloop()
```

Output:

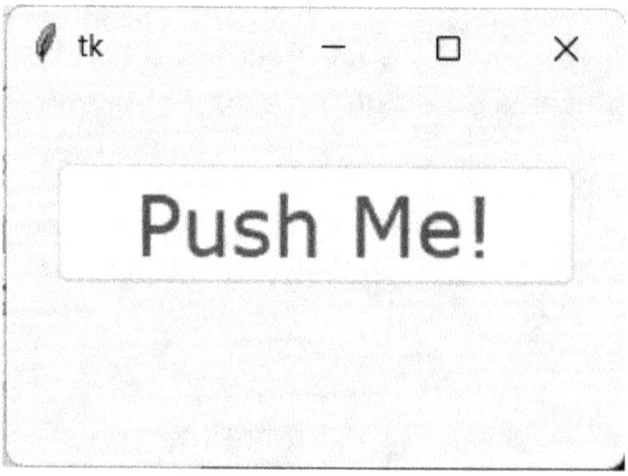

Tkinter Geometry Managers

The geometry manager controls how widgets are arranged in the window. In the simple coding examples in this book, I mainly use pack() for simplicity. For more serious projects I recommend using Grid which provides much greater control.

Tkinter has three built-in layout managers:

- Pack
- Grid
- Place

The **pack** geometry manager organizes widgets in horizontal and vertical boxes.

The **grid** geometry manager places widgets in a two dimensional grid.

The **place** geometry manager positions widgets using absolute positioning.

The Pack Geometry Manager

You may remember that I used the Pack geometry manager for my “Hello World!” example at the start of the book and its also included in many of the other examples here just because it is so easy to use.

Pack is probably the easiest to use of the three main options. While it is well worth being aware of Pack, I would recommend using the Grid geometry manager for all serious projects, the small amount of additional planning required will be rewarded.

The pack manager allows you to specify where a widget should be placed in the parent widget and how much space it should occupy. The pack manager packs widgets from top to bottom and left to right.

Using the pack manager is simple and straightforward. You just need to call the pack method on a widget, and it will be packed into the parent widget. You can use several options with the pack method to control the placement and size of the widget:

side: Specifies where the widget should be placed in the parent widget. The possible values are TOP, BOTTOM, LEFT, and RIGHT. The default value is TOP.

fill: Specifies whether the widget should expand to fill any unused space in the parent widget. The possible values are X, Y, BOTH, and NONE. The default value is NONE.

expand: Specifies whether the widget should expand to fill any extra space in the parent widget. The value is a boolean True or False. The default value is False.

padx and **pady:** Specify the amount of padding to be added on the x and y axis, respectively. The value is in pixels.

Example:

```
import tkinter as tk

root = tk.Tk()
root.geometry("200x200+100+100")

button1 = tk.Button(root, text="Top")
button1.pack(side=tk.TOP, padx=10)

button2 = tk.Button(root, text="Left")
button2.pack(side=tk.LEFT, padx=10)

button3 = tk.Button(root, text="Right")
button3.pack(side=tk.RIGHT, padx=10)

button3 = tk.Button(root, text="Bottom")
button3.pack(side=tk.BOTTOM, padx=10)

root.mainloop()
```

Output:

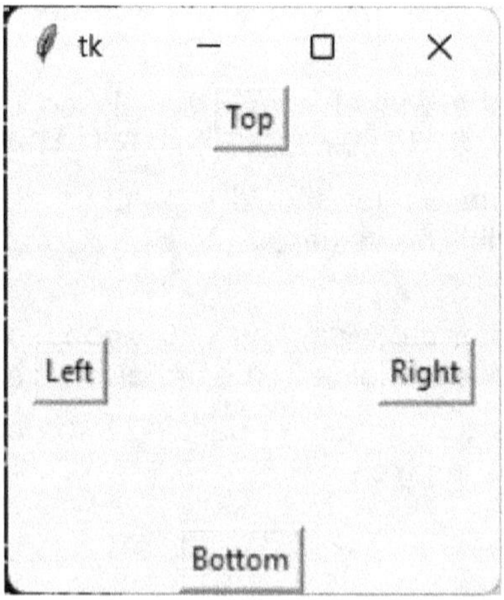

The Grid Geometry Manager

The grid geometry manager is my preferred option. Grid provides a way to arrange widgets in a table-like structure within a window. Using the grid manager, you can define rows and columns, and then place widgets into specific cells within the grid.

Within the grid, each widget is assigned a row and column value when it is created, which determines its position within the grid. The buttons are automatically resized to fit the size of their cells, and the grid itself is automatically resized to fit the size of the window.

The grid manager also supports features such as spanning multiple rows or columns, specifying row and column weights to control how the grid is resized, and controlling the padding and spacing between widgets. These features allow you to create more complex and flexible layouts for your user interfaces.

If you are planning to use grid, I suggest that you either use pen and paper or even a spreadsheet like MS Excel to draw up a grid to help you plan your layout.
Perhaps something like this:

	Column 0	Column 1	Column 2	Column 3	Column 4	Column 5
Row 0 ->						
Row 1 ->						
Row 2 ->						
Row 3 ->						
Row 4 ->						
Row 5 ->						
Row 6 ->						

Syntax:

widget.grid(row=row_index, column=column_index, , columnspan=span, sticky=stickiness)

Where:

- **widget** is the Tkinter widget you want to place in a grid.
- **row_index** is the row number in the grid where the widget should be placed.
- **column_index** is the column number in the grid where the widget should be placed.
- **columnspan** is the number of columns that the widget should span
- **stickiness** (optional) is a string that specifies how the widget should "stick" to its assigned row and column. The **stickiness** parameter can be one of the following values representing points of the compass: **N**, **S**, **E**, **W**, **NS**, **NE**, **NW**, **SE**, **SW**, **NSEW**, or **None**.

So if you want the widget to sit in the left of its assigned column, you would assign stickiness value of **W**.

A very simple example with a 3x3 grid of buttons:

```
import tkinter as tk

root = tk.Tk()

for i in range(3):
    for j in range(3):
        b = tk.Button(root, text=f"Button {i},{j}")
        b.grid(row=i, column=j)

root.mainloop()
```

Output:

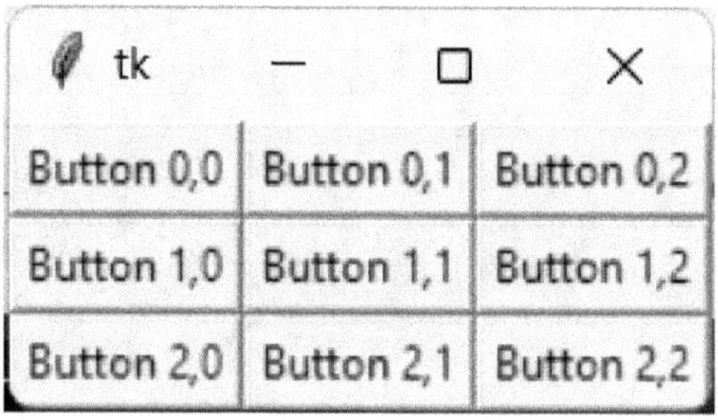

You will notice that this code contains an example of using **f-strings** to format the string. **f-strings** are a newer way to format strings in Python. They allow you to embed expressions inside string literals, using curly braces **{}**. Here is another example of this:

```
name = "John"
age = 30
print(f"My name is {name} and I am {age} years old.")
```

Now, a slightly more detailed example of using the grid geometry manager. This time I'm going to show the output first. I've made a little form to enter name and address details. In order to keep the code short I haven't changed the styles/theme etc. There are a few points worth noting:

I've used **grid_columnconfigure** to pad out the columns and set the minsize and weight first.

I've defined a function and configured some widgets to allow the tab to be used to navigate between widgets rather than just adding space.

I configured a frame and placed it within the root window **frame = ttk.Frame(root)** (you cant see it but it is there behind the buttons) this is a kind of overlay and allows me to place the three buttons independently of the columns in the root window.

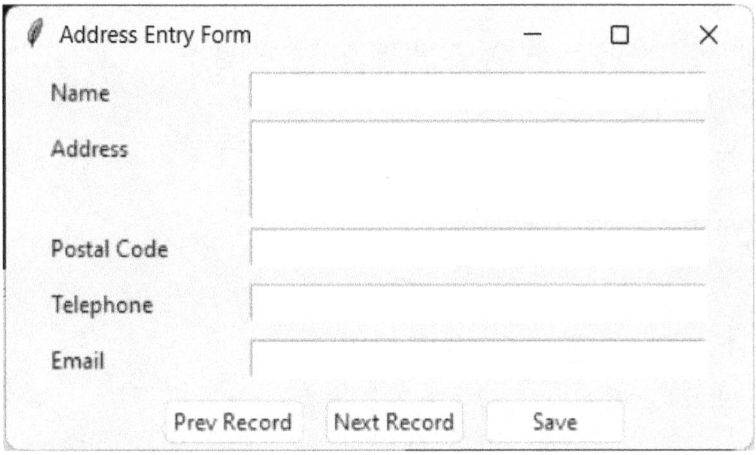

```
import tkinter as tk
import tkinter.ttk as ttk

root = tk.Tk()
root.title("Address Entry Form")
w = 400 # Window Width
h = 200 # Window Height

scrn_width = root.winfo_screenwidth()  # Width of the screen
scrn_height = root.winfo_screenheight() # Height of the screen

# Calculate Starting X and Y coordinates for Window
x = (scrn_width/2) - (w/2)
y = (scrn_height/2) - (h/2)

root.geometry('%dx%d+%d+%d' % (w, h, x, y))

def focus_next_widget(event):
        event.widget.tk_focusNext().focus()
        return("break")

for column in range(0,5):
        root.grid_columnconfigure(column, weight=1, minsize=10, pad=5)

label = ttk.Label(root, text="Name")
label.grid(row=1, column=1, sticky=W, padx=5, pady=5)
label = ttk.Label(root, text="Address")
label.grid(row=3, column=1, sticky=NW, padx=5, pady=5)
label = ttk.Label(root, text="Postal Code")
label.grid(row=7, column=1, sticky=W, padx=5, pady=5)
label = ttk.Label(root, text="Telephone")
label.grid(row=9, column=1, sticky=W, padx=5, pady=5)
label = ttk.Label(root, text="Email")
label.grid(row=11, column=1, sticky=W, padx=5, pady=5)
```

```
name = tk.Text(root, width=30, height=1)
name.grid(row=1, column=3)
address = tk.Text(root, width=30, height=3)
address.grid(row=3, column=3)
postcode = tk.Text(root, width=30, height=1)
postcode.grid(row=7, column=3)
telephone = tk.Text(root, width=30, height=1)
telephone.grid(row=9, column=3)
email = tk.Text(root, width=30, height=1)
email.grid(row=11, column=3)

# This is a frame just to hold the buttons so that
# they are aligned independently from the other widget
frame = ttk.Frame(root)
frame.grid(row=13, rowspan=3, column=1, columnspan=5)

# Note: These buttons would normally include a command option to
make
# them do something useful
button = ttk. Button(frame, text="Prev Record")
button.grid(row=1, column=3, padx=5, pady=5)
button = ttk.Button(frame, text="Next Record")
button.grid(row=1, column=4, padx=5, pady=5)
button = ttk.Button(frame, text="Save")
button.grid(row=1, column=5, padx=5, pady=5)

# These bindings allow the tab to be used to navigate between widgets
name.bind("<Tab>", focus_next_widget)
address.bind("<Tab>", focus_next_widget)
postcode.bind("<Tab>", focus_next_widget)
telephone.bind("<Tab>", focus_next_widget)
email.Bind("<Tab>", focus_next_widget)

root.mainloop()
```

The Place Geometry Manager

The place geometry manager is a way to position widgets within a window using absolute coordinates. Unlike the grid geometry manager, which arranges widgets in a table-like structure, the place manager allows you to specify the exact position and size of each widget in the window.

The place geometry manager provides fine-grained control over the layout of your user interface, *but can be more difficult to use than the grid manager*. For example, if you want to resize the window, you'll need to manually adjust the position and size of each widget to keep them in the correct location. Additionally, since the position of each widget is specified in absolute coordinates, it can be more difficult to ensure that your user interface will look good on different screen sizes and resolutions.

Read that last paragraph again. The place geometry manager is going to be difficult to manage for applications that will be used on screens of different sizes and resolutions or if the user is going to want to re-size the window (they will). It is usually preferable to stick with grid as all these factors will be handles automatically.

While place will seem appealing initially, it can become a challenge to maintain code when you need to support:

- different languages
- different operating systems
- changing fonts

Syntax:

widget.place(x=x_coordinate, y=incoordinate, width=width, height=height)

Where:

- **widget** is the Tkinter widget you want to place
- **x_coordinate** is the horizontal position of the widget, measured in pixels from the left edge of the parent widget.
- **y_coordinate** is the vertical position of the widget, measured in pixels from the top edge of the parent widget.
- **width** is the width of the widget, measured in pixels.
- **height** is the height of the widget, measured in pixels.

Example:

```
root = Tk()
root.geometry("350x300")

# Create a label widget
label = Label(root, text="Label 1")
label.place(x=50, y=50, width=100, height=25)
```

```
# Create a button widget
button = Button(root, text="Button 1")
button.place(x=200, y=50, width=100, height=50)

# Create a second label widget
label2 = Label(root, text="Label 2")
label2.place(x=50, y=150, width=100, height=25)

# Create a second button widget
button2 = Button(root, text="Button 2")
button2.place(x=200, y=150, width=100, height=50)
root.mainloop()
```

Output:

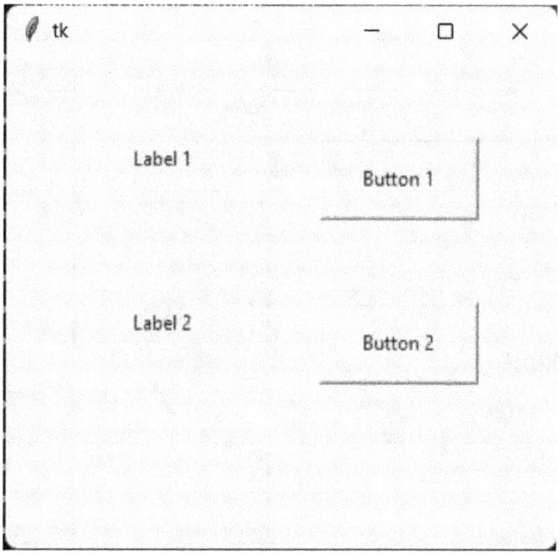

Widgets

All of the elements of the GUI (labels, buttons, etc) are known as Widgets. Tkinter includes widgets for the basic elements that you will find in most user interfaces as well as a few more advanced ones.

Here is a table of both the standard Tkinter widgets and ttk widgets in alphabetical order. Remember that you can mix and match both types in the same app/GUI! :

Widget	Tkinter	ttk
Button	✓	✓
Canvas	✓	NO
Checkbutton	✓	✓
Combobox	NO	✓
Entry	✓	✓
Frame	✓	✓
Label	✓	✓
LabelFrame	✓	✓
Listbox	✓	✓
Menu	✓	NO
Menubutton	✓	NO
Message	✓	✓
Notebook	NO	✓
OptionMenu	✓	NO
PanedWindow	✓	NO
Progressbar	✓	✓
Radiobutton	✓	✓
Scale	✓	✓
Scrollbar	✓	✓
Separator	NO	✓
Sizegrip	NO	✓
Spinbox	✓	✓
Text	✓	✓
Treeview	NO	✓

Later in this book I will explain the basic syntax and features for each in turn. For ease of later reference, I'll cover them in alphabetical order.

Ttk comes with 18 widgets, twelve of which already existed in tkinter: Button, Checkbutton, Entry, Frame, Label, LabelFrame, Menubutton, PanedWindow, Radiobutton, Scale, Scrollbar, and Spinbox. The other six are new for ttk: Combobox, Notebook, Progressbar, Separator, Sizegrip and Treeview.

Button

The purpose of the standard Button widget is fairly obvious, a button is displayed which when pressed triggers a command. The button itself can display text or an image and has many visual characteristics which can be adjusted both by direct parameters and in the case of the ttk Buttons also by styles and themes.

As the first widget that I'm looking at (alphabetically), I will take a little more in depth look at the button widget than at some of the others.

Syntax:

my_btn = Button(parent, text="press me", option, option, etc)

my_btn.pack() # or whatever geometry manager you are using

Where parent = parent window such as root or window

Some popular parameters are show in the table below. This list may not be exhaustive.

Option	Description
activebackground	The background colour of the button when it is active.
activeforeground	The text colour of the button when it is active.
anchor	Specifies the position of the text inside the button.
background (or "bg")	The background colour of the button.
bitmap	The bitmap image to be displayed on the button.
borderwidth (or "bd")	The width of the border around the button.
command	The function to be executed when the button is clicked.
compound	Specifies the positioning of the text and image inside the button.
cursor	The cursor that appears when the mouse is over the button.
default	Specifies whether the button should be the default button on the form.
disabledforeground	The text colour of the button when it is

	disabled.
font	The font used for the button text.
foreground (or "fg")	The colour of the button text.
height	The height of the button.
highlightbackground	The colour of the button's highlight border when it does not have focus.
highlightcolor	The colour of the button's highlight border when it has focus.
highlightthickness	The thickness of the button's highlight border.
image	The image to be displayed on the button.
justify	Specifies the alignment of the button text.
padx	The horizontal padding around the button text and image.
pady	The vertical padding around the button text and image.
relief	The border style of the button (e.g. "raised", "sunken", "flat", "groove", "ridge").
repeatdelay	The delay (in milliseconds) before repeating the button click when the button is held down.
repeatinterval	The interval (in milliseconds) between repeated button clicks when the button is held down.
state	Specifies whether the button is enabled or disabled.
takefocus	Specifies whether the button can be given focus.
text	The text to be displayed on the button.
textvariable	The text variable to be displayed on the button.
underline	Specifies which character in the button text should be underlined.
width	The width of the button.

Example:

```
import tkinter as tk

root = tk.Tk()
```

```
root.geometry("300x100")

# Define a function to be called when the button is clicked
def button_clicked():
    print("Button clicked!")

# Create a button widget with optional parameters
button = tk.Button(root, text="Click Me", font=("Arial", 14), bg="lightblue",
fg="white", command=button_clicked)

# Set the position and size of the button using the geometry manager
button.pack(padx=10, pady=10)

# Start the main event loop
root.mainloop()
```

In this example, we create a Button widget with the following optional parameters:

text the label for the button

font the font to use for the label

bg the background colour of the button

fg the text colour of the label

command the function to call when the button is clicked

We also use the pack geometry manager to set the position and size of the button.

When you run this code, a window will appear with a button labelled "Click Me". When you click the button, the function button_clicked will be called and the message "Button clicked!" will be printed to the console.

Button (ttk)

While the standard button is very easy to use if you just want one or two, if you are going to be using a lot of buttons it makes sense to create a style or two and used the ttk themed buttons.

Syntax:

The simplest option is something like:

button = ttk.Button(root, text='Click me!', command=button_clicked)

which would change the default style of TButton (themed button). If you wanted to create your own style called “**my_button**” changing the font and colours from the default:

style = ttk.Style()

style.configure('my_button.TButton', font=('Helvetica', 14), foreground='blue', background='#e6e6e6', padding=10)

which could then be used as follows:

button1 = ttk.Button(root, text="Click me", style="my_button.TButton", command=my_command)

Options:

Option	Description
text	The label to display on the button
image	An image to display on the button
compound	How to display the image and text on the button ("left", "right", "top", or "bottom")
command	The function to call when the button is clicked
state	The state of the button ("normal", "disabled", "readonly")
style	The style of the button
takefocus	Whether the button can be selected with the keyboard
underline	The index of the character in the text to underline
width	The width of the button (in characters)
padding	The amount of padding around the button contents (in pixels)
default	Whether the button is the default button in a dialog
cursor	The mouse cursor to use when the mouse is over the button
class_	The widget class for the button
textvariable	A StringVar or IntVar that stores the button's text
image	An image to display on the button
overrelief	The relief style to use when the mouse is over the button
repeatdelay	The delay in milliseconds before a button press is repeated
repeatinterval	The interval in milliseconds between button press repeats
cursor	The mouse cursor to use when the mouse is over the button
underline	The index of the character in the text to underline
padding	The amount of padding around the button contents

	(in pixels)

Example:

```
import tkinter as tk
from tkinter import ttk

root = tk.Tk()
root.geometry("250x150")
root.title("Themed Button")

style = ttk.Style() # create a style for the button
style.configure('mybutton.TButton', font=('Arial', 18), foreground='blue',
overrelief='solid', padding=20, underline=0)

# create a button with the custom style
button = ttk.Button(root, text="Click me", style='mybutton.TButton')
button.pack(pady=20)
root.mainloop()
```

Output:

Canvas

The Canvas widget in Tkinter is a container for graphical elements, such as lines, arcs, text, and images. The Tkinter Canvas widget is a rectangular area where you can draw graphics, such as lines, arcs, circles, and text, or place images. It is a powerful and flexible widget that provides a way to create complex and interactive graphical user interfaces.

Some of the features of the Tkinter Canvas widget include:

- **Drawing** The Canvas widget allows you to draw various shapes, such as lines, rectangles, circles, arcs, polygons, and text. You can set the colours, line widths, fill patterns, and fonts for these shapes. You can also move, resize, and delete these shapes.
- **Image handling** You can display images on the canvas using the **create_image** method. The images can be in GIF, PPM, or PNG format.
- **Event handling** The Canvas widget can handle mouse and keyboard events. You can bind mouse and keyboard events to shapes on the canvas or to the entire canvas. For example, you can bind a mouse click event to a rectangle, so that the rectangle changes colour when you click on it.
- **Scaling and scrolling** You can scale and scroll the canvas contents, which is useful when working with large or complex drawings.
- **Tags** You can add tags to shapes on the canvas, which allows you to group and manipulate them as a single entity.

You can use the Canvas widget to create interactive visualizations or drawing applications. The Canvas widget provides methods for drawing shapes and text, as well as for handling mouse and keyboard events.

You can also create custom objects on the canvas by subclassing the Canvas widget and implementing custom drawing methods. Overall, the Canvas widget is a versatile tool for creating graphical applications in Tkinter.

Syntax Example:

```
import tkinter as tk
root = tk.Tk()
canvas = tk.Canvas(root, width=400, height=300)
canvas.pack()
root.mainloop()
```

There are a number of **Canvas.create** methods used to draw on the Canvas

- Canvas.create_arc()
- Canvas.create_bitmap()
- Canvas.create_image()
- Canvas.create_line()
- Canvas.create_oval()
- Canvas.create_polygon()
- Canvas.create_rectangle()
- Canvas.create_text()

- Canvas.create_window()

Here are the common arguments that you can use with the Canvas widget's create methods in Tkinter:

- activefill
- activewidth
- anchor
- dash
- dashoffset
- disableddash
- disabledfill
- disabledoutline
- fill
- font
- outline
- smooth
- splinesteps
- state
- stipple
- tags
- width
- joinstyle
- capstyle

Not all of these arguments are applicable to every create method - some are specific to certain types of objects, such as font for text objects or joinstyle for line objects.

Canvas is a very powerful widget which could be used to create powerful graphics packages and could justify a book on it's own. Here is a simple example to draw a house:

```
import tkinter as tk

# Create a canvas with a white background
root = tk.Tk()
canvas = tk.Canvas(root, width=400, height=400, bg="white")
canvas.pack()

# Draw the house
canvas.create_rectangle(100, 250, 300, 400, fill="light blue")  # main
house
canvas.create_rectangle(150, 300, 250, 400, fill="white") # door
canvas.create_oval(180, 330, 200, 350, fill="yellow") # door knob
canvas.create_polygon(100, 250, 200, 150, 300, 250, fill="red") # roof
```

```
canvas.create_rectangle(170, 320, 190, 350, fill="white") # window 1
canvas.create_rectangle(210, 320, 230, 350, fill="white") # window 2

# Run the application
root.mainloop()
```

Output (imagine the colours if you have a mono version of the book)! :

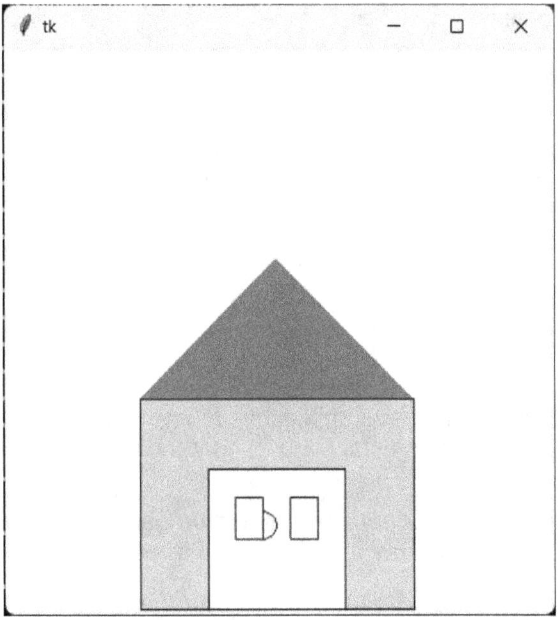

Checkbutton

Checkbutton is a widget used to create a simple checkbox that can be selected or deselected by the user.

Some of the common options are **variable** (which can be used to associate a Tkinter variable with the Checkbutton), **onvalue** and **offvalue** (which specify the values to use when the Checkbutton is checked or unchecked), **command** (which specifies a function to be called when the Checkbutton is clicked), and **state** (which can be set to NORMAL, DISABLED, or ACTIVE to control whether the Checkbutton is clickable or not).

Syntax:

my_checkbutton = Checkbutton(root, option, option etc)

Options:

Option	Description

text	sets the label of the checkbox.
variable	sets the Tkinter variable associated with the checkbox. When the checkbox is checked, the variable will be set to a value of 1; when it is unchecked, the variable will be set to 0.
onvalue	sets the value to be assigned to the variable when the checkbox is checked.
offvalue	sets the value to be assigned to the variable when the checkbox is unchecked.
command	sets the function to be called when the checkbox is clicked.

Example:

```
import tkinter as tk

root = tk.Tk()
root.geometry("250x50")
root.title("Checkbutton Example")

# Create a Checkbutton
my_checkbutton = tk.Checkbutton(root, text="Select me",
font="Helvetica 14")

# Pack the Checkbutton into the window
my_checkbutton.pack()

# Run the main loop
root.mainloop()
```

Output:

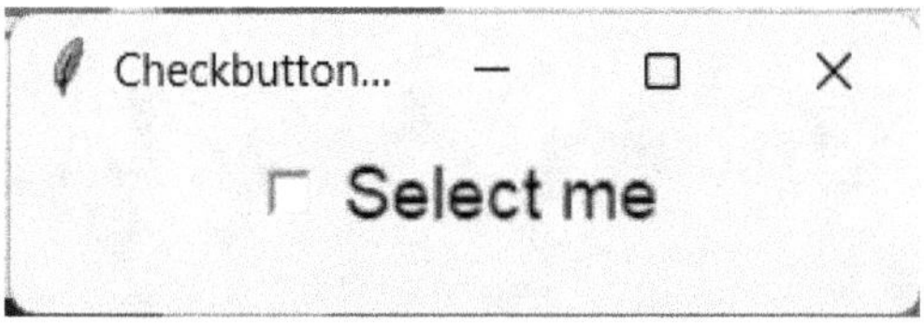

Colorchooser

OK, not strictly a widget, the Tkinter **colorchooser** module uses the native colour chooser dialog box. This package has a function **askcolor()** that when called it makes the color chooser dialogue box pop up. The function returns the hexadecimal code of the color selected by the user. Apologies for the spelling of color/colour.

Syntax:

colorchooser.askcolor()

Example:

```
import tkinter as tk
from tkinter import ttk
from tkinter.colorchooser import askcolor

root = tk.Tk()
root.title('Tkinter Colour Chooser')
root.geometry('250x200')

def choose_colour():
    colours = askcolor(title="Tkinter Colour Chooser")
    root.configure(bg=colours[1])

ttk.Button(root, text='Select a Colour',
command=choose_colour).pack(expand=True)

root.mainloop()
```

Combobox (ttk)

The ttk.Combobox widget is a useful tool for creating user interfaces that allow the user to select from a list of options or enter their own value in a text field. It combines the features of a standard Entry widget with a Listbox widget, making it a useful tool for data entry or selection.

The ttk.Combobox widget has several optional parameters that can be used to customize its appearance and behaviour, including:

- **values** a list of values to display in the drop-down list
- **state** determines whether the user can type in the Combobox or only select from the list ("readonly")
- **width** the width of the Combobox in characters
- **font** the font used to display the text in the Combobox

In addition, the ttk.Combobox widget has several methods that can be used to interact with its state, such as:

- **current()** returns the current selection in the Combobox
- **set()** sets the selection in the Combobox to the specified value
- **get()** returns the value currently displayed in the Combobox text field

Example which includes a custom style for the Combobox:

```
import tkinter as tk
from tkinter import ttk

root = tk.Tk()
root.geometry("300x200")

# Define a custom style for the combobox
style = ttk.Style()
style.theme_create("custom_style", parent="alt", settings={
    "TCombobox": {
        "configure": {
            "selectbackground": "blue",
            "fieldbackground": "white",
            "background": "white",
            "foreground": "black",
            "arrowcolor": "black",
            "arrowpadding": 4,
            "padding": 4,
            "bordercolor": "lightblue",
```

```
            "borderwidth": 1,
            "relief": "solid",
            "font": ("Arial", 12)
        }
    }
})
style.theme_use("custom_style")

# Define the values for the combobox
values = ["Option 1", "Option 2", "Option 3", "Option 4"]

# Create a combobox widget with custom style
combobox = ttk.Combobox(root, values=values, state="readonly",
width=20, font=("Arial", 12))

# Set the position and size of the combobox using the geometry
manager
combobox.pack(pady=20)

# Start the main event loop
root.mainloop()
```

Entry

The Entry widget provides a single-line text field (When entering a large quantity of text I tend to use the multi-line **Text** widget instead) which can be used to enter a string.

Syntax:

my_entry = Entry(root, options)

Some of the common options are **width** (which specifies the width of the widget in characters), **show** (which can be set to a character to mask the input, e.g. for password entry), and **textvariable** (which can be used to associate a **StringVar** or **IntVar** with the widget to get or set its value).

A simple password entry example:

```
import tkinter as tk

root = tk.Tk()
root.geometry("300x50")
root.title("Password Entry")

# Create a StringVar to store the value of the Entry widget
my_var = tk.StringVar()

label = Label(text="Enter your password and press Enter")
label.pack()

# Create an Entry widget with custom options
entry = tk.Entry(root, width=30, textvariable=my_var, show="*")

# Set the initial value of the StringVar
my_var.set("Enter your password here...")

# Define a function to be called when the Enter key is pressed
def on_return_key(event):
    print(my_var.get())

# Bind the function to the Enter key
entry.bind("<Return>", on_return_key)

entry.pack()
```

```
root.mainloop()
```

Output:

Frame

Frame is a widget that acts as a container for other widgets. It is a rectangular area that can hold other widgets, such as buttons, labels, and entry widgets. The Frame widget helps to organise the layout as it is used to group other widgets together in a window or dialog box.

One of the main advantages of using a Frame widget is that it allows you to group related widgets together and apply layout management to them as a group.

Syntax:

my_frame = Frame(parent, options)

The Frame widget provides several options that can be used to customise its appearance and behaviour. Some of the common options are **width** and **height** (which specify the size of the widget), **borderwidth** and **relief** (which control the border style), padx and pady (which add padding to the widget), and background or bg (which set the background color).

relief options are:

- **FLAT** This option provides a flat border with no relief.
- **RAISED** This option gives the frame a raised appearance, making it look like it is sticking out of the screen.
- **SUNKEN** This option gives the frame a sunken appearance, making it look like it is pushed into the screen.
- **GROOVE** This option gives the frame a 3D groove effect.
- **RIDGE** This option gives the frame a 3D ridge effect.

Example:

```
import tkinter as tk

root = tk.Tk()
root.geometry("300x200")

# Create a Frame to group the widgets
frame = Frame(root, bd=5, relief='raised', padx=10, pady=10)
frame.pack(side='top', fill='x')

# Add labels and buttons to the Frame
Label(frame, text='Grouped Widgets', font=('Arial', 16)).pack(pady=10)
Label(frame, text='Label 1').pack()
Label(frame, text='Label 2').pack()
Button(frame, text='Button 1').pack(pady=5)
Button(frame, text='Button 2').pack(pady=5)

root.mainloop()
```

Output:

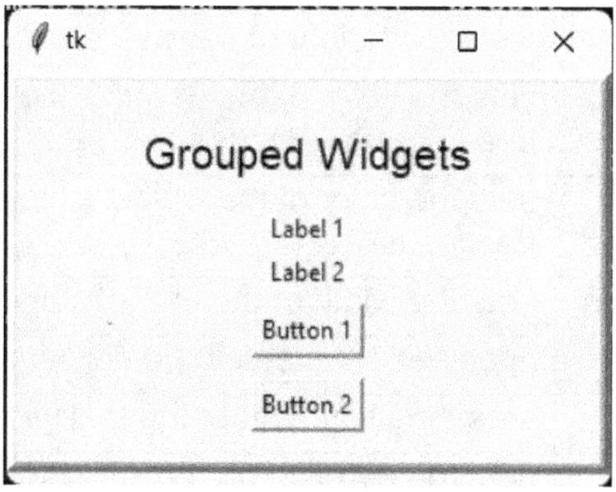

Label

Label widget is one of the most basic GUI elements that is used to display text and images. It can be used to display static text or to create a text label for other widgets such as buttons or entry fields.

Syntax:

my_label = Label(parent, options)

Options:

Some of the most common options for the Label widget include:

Option	Description
anchor	sets the position of the text within the widget (N, NE, E, SE, S, SW, W, NW, or CENTER).
bg or background	sets the background color of the widget.
bd or borderwidth	sets the width of the widget's border.
bitmap	specifies a bitmap to be displayed on the widget.
compound	specifies how the image and text should be combined on the widget.
cursor	sets the cursor to be displayed when the mouse is over the widget.
font	sets the font used to display text on the widget.
fg or foreground	sets the foreground color of the widget.
height	sets the height of the widget.
highlightbackground	sets the color of the widget's highlight when it does not have focus.
highlightcolor	sets the color of the widget's highlight when it has focus.
highlightthickness	sets the width of the widget's highlight.
image	specifies an image to be displayed on the widget.
justify	sets the alignment of the text within the widget.
padx	sets the padding on the left and right sides of the widget.
pady	sets the padding on the top and bottom sides of the widget.
relief	sets the type of border to be displayed around the widget.
state	sets the state of the widget (normal, active, or disabled).
takefocus	specifies whether the widget should be included

	in the focus order.
text	sets the text to be displayed on the widget.
textvariable	specifies a Tkinter variable to hold the text displayed on the widget.
underline	sets the index of the character that should be underlined in the widget's text.
width	sets the width of the widget.
wraplength	sets the maximum line length for the widget's text. If set to 0, wrapping is disabled.

A nice simple example:

```
import tkinter as tk

root = tk.Tk()

label = Label(root, text="Hello World!", font="Arial 24", fg="blue",
bg="yellow").pack()

root.mainloop()
```

Output (if you don't have a colour copy, the text is blue on a yellow background):

Label – Displaying an image

The Label widget (in fact the ttk.Label widget in the example below) can be used to display images as well as text.

Here is a simple example:

```
import tkinter as tk
from tkinter import ttk

root = tk.Tk()
root.geometry("500x400")
root.title("Themed Label")
```

```
myimage = tk.PhotoImage(file=r"C:\Users\racer.gif")

label = ttk.Label(root, image=myimage)
label.pack()

root.mainloop()
```

There are a couple of important points to be aware of here:

- Where the file path is included, the r stands for "raw" and will cause backslashes in the string to be interpreted as actual backslashes rather than special characters as would otherwise be the case with Python
- The **PhotoImage** class can only handle GIF, PGM, and PPM image file types. If you want to use other image file types such as JPEG or PNG, you need to use the Python Imaging Library (PIL) or its fork, Pillow, to load and convert the image file.

Output:

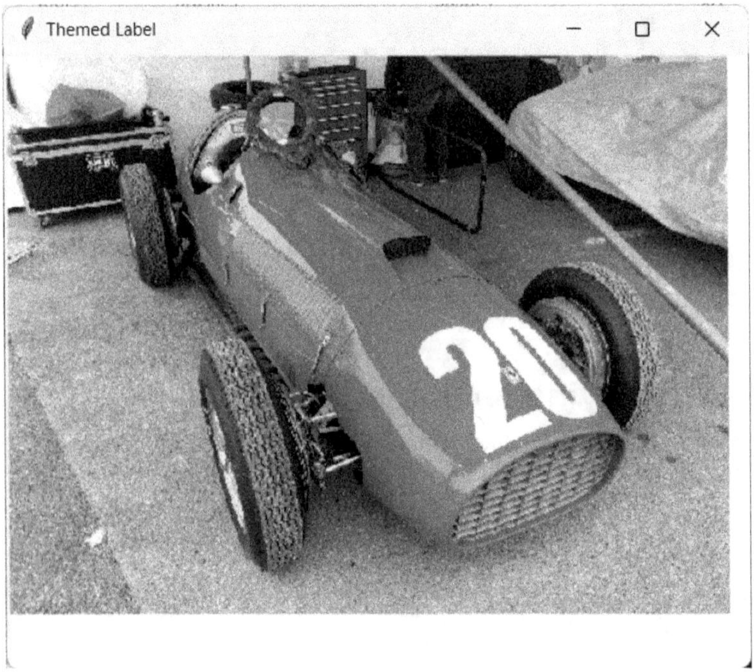

LabelFrame

The LabelFrame widget provides a frame with a label. It is used to group and organize other widgets within a window.

The LabelFrame widget has a rectangular frame with a label at the top.

Syntax:

my_labelframe = LabelFrame(parent, options)

Options:

Option	Description
text	specifies the text that will be displayed as the label on top of the LabelFrame.
labelanchor	This option specifies the position of the label in the LabelFrame. It can be set to one of the following values n, s, e, w, nw, ne, sw, or se. The default value is nw (northwest).
bg or background	sets the background colour of the LabelFrame.
fg or foreground	sets the text color of the label on the LabelFrame.
relief	specifies the type of border that should be drawn around the LabelFrame. The possible values are flat, raised, sunken, groove, and ridge.
borderwidth or bd	specifies the width of the border around the LabelFrame.
padx and pady	These options specify the padding around the contents of the LabelFrame.
width and height	These options specify the width and height of the LabelFrame.
highlightthickness	specifies the width of the highlight border around the LabelFrame when it has the keyboard focus.
highlightbackground	sets the color of the highlight border around the LabelFrame.
highlightcolor	sets the colour of the focus highlight ring when the LabelFrame has focus.

Example:

```
from tkinter import *

win = Tk()
win.geometry("300x100")

my_labelframe = LabelFrame(win, text="This is a labelframe",
font="Helvetica 18", borderwidth=5, relief="raised")
my_labelframe.pack(fill="both", expand="yes")

my_label = Label(my_labelframe, text="This is the label text", font="Arial
24")
my_label.pack()

win.mainloop()
```

Output

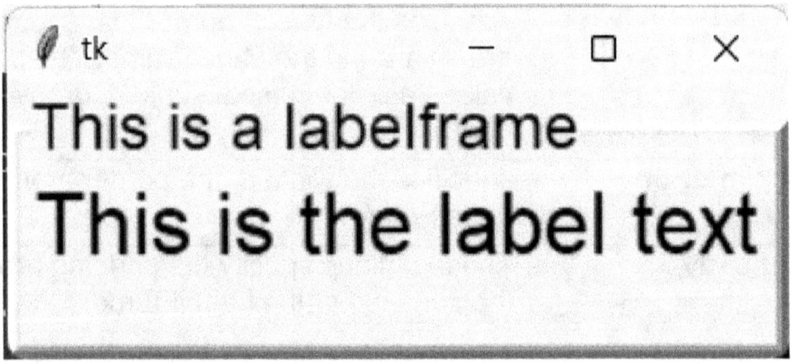

Listbox

Listbox is a widget that displays a list of items from which the user can select one or more items.

syntax:

my_listbox = Listbox(parent, options)

Options include:

Option	Description
bg	The background color of the widget.
bd	The border width of the widget.
cursor	The cursor to be displayed when the mouse is over the widget.
exportselection	A boolean value that indicates whether the current selection should be exported to the clipboard.
fg	The foreground color (i.e., text colour) of the widget.
font	The font used to display the text in the widget.
height	The number of visible items in the listbox.
highlightcolor	The color of the highlight rectangle that is displayed when an item is selected.
highlightthickness	The thickness of the highlight rectangle.
listvariable	A variable that contains a list of strings to be displayed in the listbox.
relief	The border style of the widget ("flat", "groove", "raised", "ridge", "solid", or "sunken").
selectbackground	The background color of the selected items.
selectmode	The selection mode, which can be either "SINGLE", "BROWSE" (only one item can be selected at a time, but the selection can be cleared), "MULTIPLE" (multiple items can be selected at the same time), or "EXTENDED" (like "MULTIPLE", but the selection can be extended by dragging the mouse).
Width	The width of the widget in characters.

A simple example:

```
import tkinter as tk

root = tk.Tk()
root.geometry("350x200")

my_list=["Monday", "Tuesday", "Wednesday", "Thursday", "Friday",
"Saturday", "Sunday"]

my_listbox = tk.Listbox(root, font="Arial 14", listvariable =
tk.StringVar(value=my_list))
my_listbox.pack()

root.mainloop()
```

Output:

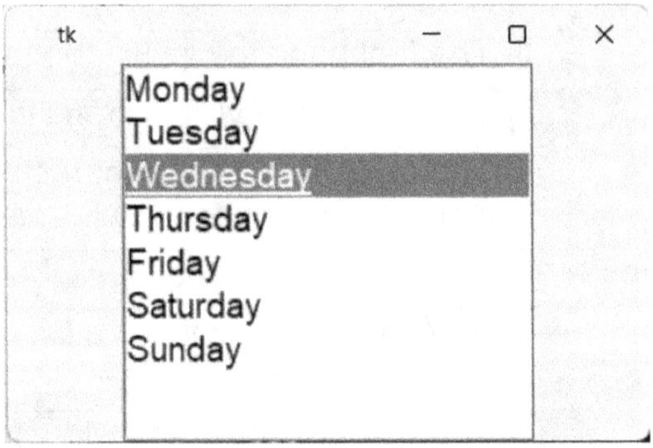

Menus and Menubars

A menu is one of the best known and most useful widgets when creating a GUI. Along with Buttons, selecting menu items is one of the best ways for a user action on the GUI to trigger a command.

Syntax:

my_menu = Menu(parent, options)

Tkinter menus could potentially be a big subject. Not that they are particularly complex – you should get the idea from taking a look at my example below.

The standard type of Menu that I have shown is basically made up of three parts:

- The Menubar
- The Cascade (the columns that open from each item on the menubar)
- The Commands (the labelled options that trigger a command)

my_menubar = Menu(root)

This creates a menubar and assigns it to a parent window (root in this case).

firstmenu = Menu(my_menubar) # first column

I think of this as creating a menu on the menubar

my_menubar.add_cascade(label="File", menu=firstmenu)

This then uses the **.add_cascade** method adds a 'cascade' (like a dropdown) from the menubar headed by a label ("File" in this case – often the first menu option in a window)

firstmenu.add_command(label="File menu item1", command=my_command)

The **.add_command** method adds named items to the cascade each with a named command. You can separate these with an **.add_separator()** if required as in the example below.

Example:

```
from tkinter import *

def quit():
    root.destroy()

root = tk.Tk()
root.title("Example Menu Program")
root.geometry("400x200+100+200")
root.option_add("*tearOff", False) # prevents the tear off

my_menubar = Menu(root)
firstmenu = Menu(my_menubar) # first column
my_menubar.add_cascade(label="File", menu=firstmenu)
firstmenu.add_command(label="File menu item1")
firstmenu.add_command(label="File menu item2")
firstmenu.add_command(label="File menu item3")
firstmenu.add_separator()
firstmenu.add_command(label="Quit", command=quit)
secondmenu = Menu(my_menubar) # second column
my_menubar.add_cascade(label="Stuff", menu=secondmenu)
secondmenu.add_command(label="Stuff One")
secondmenu.add_command(label="Stuff Two")
secondmenu.add_command(label="Stuff Three")
thirdmenu = Menu(my_menubar) # third column
my_menubar.add_cascade(label="More Stuff", menu=thirdmenu)
thirdmenu.add_command(label="More Stuff One")
thirdmenu.add_command(label="More Stuff Two")
thirdmenu.add_command(label="More Stuff Three")

root.config(menu=my_menubar)
root.mainloop()
```

Output:

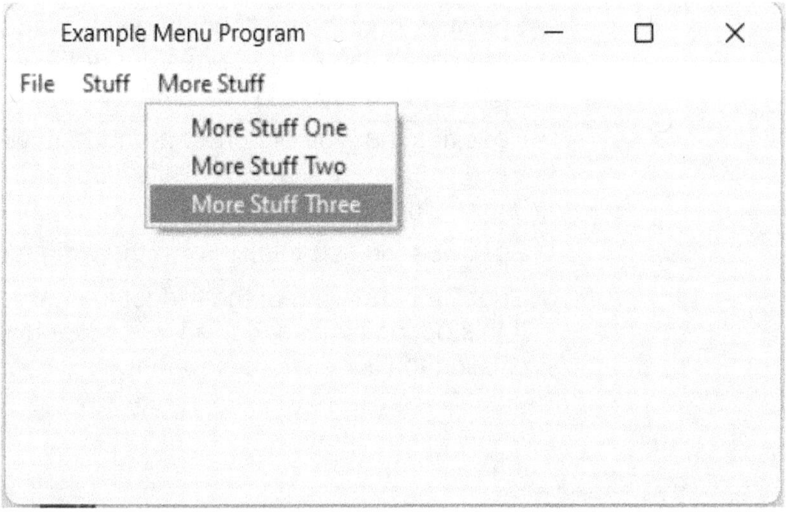

As this is just a simple example, I haven't assigned commands to any of the menu options other than quit.

Message

The Message widget is used to display a short message to the user. It is similar to the Label widget, but it automatically wraps text to fit within the specified width.

Syntax:

my_message = Message(parent, options)

Options:

Option	Description
anchor	Specifies how the text should be aligned within the widget. Valid values are "n", "s", "e", "w", "nw", "ne", "sw", "se", and "center". The default is "nw".
bg/background	background colour of the widget.
bd/borderwidth	Specifies the width of the border around the widget. The default value is 2 pixels.
font	the font to use for the text in the widget.
fg/foreground	the colour of the text in the widget.
highlightbackground	Specifies the colour of the highlight border when the widget does not have focus.
highlightcolor	Specifies the colour of the highlight when the widget has focus.

highlightthickness	the width of the highlight border.
justify	Specifies how the text should be justified within each line. Valid values are "left", "center", and "right". The default is "left".
relief	Specifies the type of border around the widget. Valid values are "flat", "raised", "sunken", "solid", "ridge", and "groove".
text	Specifies the text to display in the widget.
width	Specifies the width of the widget in characters. If this option is not specified, the widget will expand to fill the available width.

Example:

```
import tkinter as tk

root = tk.Tk()
root.geometry("250x50")
root.title("Message")

message = tk.Message(root, text="This is a message", width=100,
font=("Arial", 12), fg="blue")
message.pack()

root.mainloop()
```

Output:

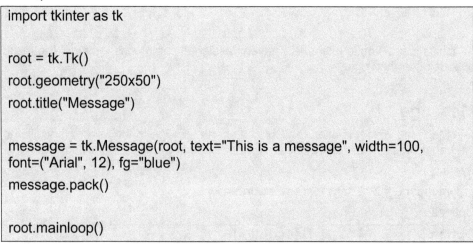

Notebook (ttk)

The Notebook widget in tkinter provides a tabbed interface in the GUI for organising and displaying multiple widgets. Notebook Tabs are similar to the tabs in a web browser or a spreadsheet application.

There are a few steps to create a Notebook:

- Create the Notebook
- Create child widgets / tabs
- Add the child widgets to the Notebook

Syntax:

my_notebook = ttk.Notebook(parent, options)

my_frame = ttk.Frame(my_notebook)

my_label = ttk.Label(my_frame, text="This is a frame in a notebook")

my_notebook.add(my_frame, text="Text in Frame")

my_notebook.pack() # or other method of geometry management

Child widgets are added to the Notebook using the **add**() method, which takes the child widget and a name for the tab as arguments.

You can specify various options for each tab, such as the background color, foreground (text) color, and font.

The Notebook widget emits an event whenever the user switches tabs, which you can handle using the **bind()** method.

Options:

Option	Description
height	Specifies the height of the widget in pixels.
width	Specifies the width of the widget in pixels.
padding	Specifies the padding between the tabs and the contents of the widget.
style	Specifies the style to use for the widget.
takefocus	Specifies whether the widget can receive keyboard focus.
tabposition	Specifies the position of the tabs. Valid values are "n" (north), "s" (south), "e" (east), and "w" (west).
tabs	Specifies a list of dictionaries that define the tabs. Each dictionary must have a "text" key that specifies the text to display on the tab, and can also include

	other keys such as "image" (to specify an image to display on the tab), "compound" (to specify whether to display the image and text together or separately), and "state" (to specify whether the tab is enabled or disabled).

Example:

```
import tkinter as tk
from tkinter import ttk

root = tk.Tk()
root.geometry("250x200")
root.title("Notebook")

my_notebook = ttk.Notebook(root)

frame_1 = ttk.Frame(my_notebook)
label_1 = ttk.Label(frame_1, text="This is frame 1").pack()
frame_2 = ttk.Frame(my_notebook)
label_2 = ttk.Label(frame_2, text="This is frame 2").pack()
frame_3 = ttk.Frame(my_notebook)
label_3 = ttk.Label(frame_3, text="This is frame 3").pack()

my_notebook.add(frame_1, text="Frame 1") # add frames to Notebook
my_notebook.add(frame_2, text="Frame 2")
my_notebook.add(frame_3, text="Frame 3")

my_notebook.pack() # pack the Notebook to display it on the screen

root.mainloop()
```

Output:

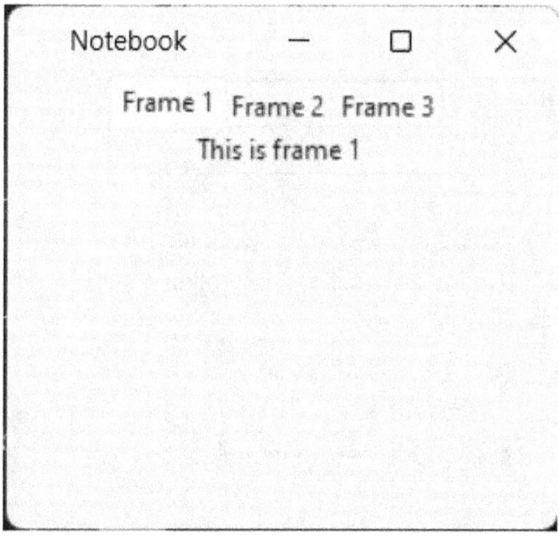

Depending on how well this is printed, it may not be clear – There are three Tabs in the Notebook labelled “Frame 1”, “Frame 2” and “Frame 3”. The “Frame 1” tab is selected in the Notebook and therefore we see the text “This is frame 1”. Hopefully this is clear in the code.

OptionMenu

OptionMenu is a GUI widget that provides a drop-down menu of options to the user. It allows the user to select one option from a list of predefined options. As the number of options available varies, the syntax is slightly more complex than usual.

Syntax:

my_optionmenu = OptionMenu(parent, selected_option, *options_list)

where

options_list is something like options_list = [‘Option 1’, ‘Option 2’, ‘Option 3’]

and

selected_option is a tkinter StringVar variable to store the selected option

The asterisk (*) before the **options_list** variable in the **OptionMenu** widget constructor is called the "unpacking operator" or "splat operator".

In this context, the * is used to unpack the elements of the **options_list** into individual arguments to the **OptionMenu**.

Without the * operator, the **OptionMenu** constructor would receive a single argument, which would be the **options_list** list. But since the **OptionMenu** constructor expects a variable number of arguments, we need to use the * operator to unpack the list and pass its elements as separate arguments.

Hopefully this example will make things a little clearer:

```
import tkinter as tk

root = tk.Tk()
root.geometry("250x100")
root.title("OptionMenu")

# Define a list of options to be displayed in the OptionMenu
option_list = ["Option 1", "Option 2", "Option 3", "Option 4"]

# Create a variable to store the selected option
selected_option = tk.StringVar(root)
selected_option.set(option_list[0])  # set the default option

# the * is used to unpack the elements of the option_list
option_menu = tk.OptionMenu(root, selected_option, *option_list).pack()

# Create a label to display the selected option
selected_label = tk.Label(root, textvariable=selected_option).pack()

root.mainloop()
```

Output:

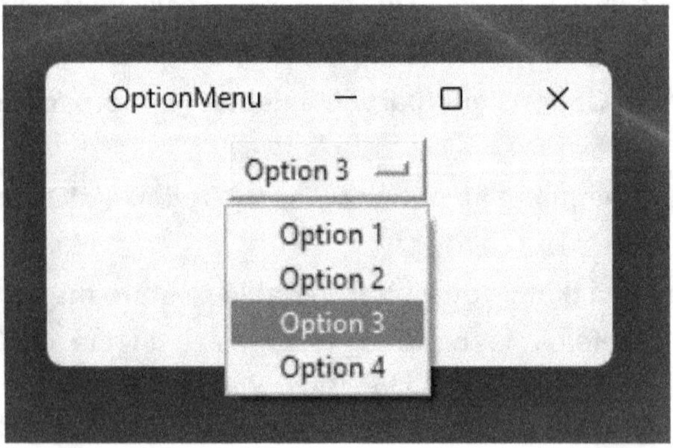

PanedWindow

PanedWindow allows the user to split the window horizontally or vertically into resizable panes, each of which can contain other widgets. The PanedWindow widget can be used to create a split pane user interface for an application, the user can adjust the size of each pane by dragging the divider that separates them.

Syntax:

Create a PanedWindow

paned_window = PanedWindow(parent, orient=HORIZONTAL)

(orientation can also be VERTICAL)

create frames for the PanedWindow

left_frame = Frame(paned_window)

paned_window.add(left_frame)

right_frame = Frame(paned_window)

paned_window.add(right_frame)

Pack the PanedWindow in the root window

paned_window.pack(fill=BOTH, expand=1)

Syntax Example where a paned window is created and Label widgets are added to the left and right Frames:

```
from tkinter import *

root = Tk()
root.geometry("300x200")
paned_window = PanedWindow(root, orient=HORIZONTAL)
paned_window.pack(fill=BOTH, expand=1)

left_frame = Frame(paned_window, bg="red")
paned_window.add(left_frame)

right_frame = Frame(paned_window, bg="green")
paned_window.add(right_frame)

left_label = Label(left_frame, text="Left Label")
left_label.pack(side=tk.LEFT, padx=10)
```

```
right_label = Label(right_frame, text="right Label")
right_label.pack(side=tk.RIGHT, padx=10)

root.mainloop()
```

Output:

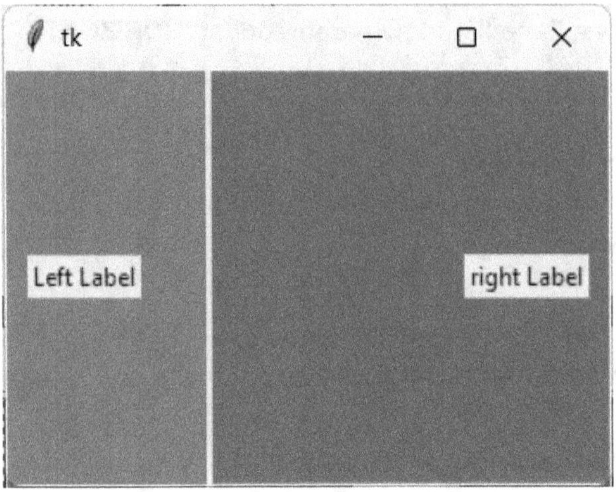

Progressbar (ttk)

The Progressbar widget can be used to display the progress of an operation, such as a file download or data processing task. It could also be used to represent how a value sites within a predetermined range.

Syntax:

progress = ttk.Progressbar(parent, options)

Options

Option	Description
orient	sets the orientation of the progress bar (HORIZONTAL or VERTICAL).
mode	sets the mode of the progress bar (determinate, indeterminate, or determinate/indeterminate).
maximum	sets the maximum value of the progress bar.
value	sets the value of the progress bar.
length	sets the length of the progress bar (in pixels).
variable	specifies a Tkinter variable to hold the value of the progress bar.

maximum	sets the maximum value.
minimum	sets the minimum value.
orient	sets the orientation of the progress bar (HORIZONTAL or VERTICAL).
style	specifies the style of the progress bar.
thickness	sets the thickness of the progress bar (in pixels).
mode	sets the mode of the progress bar (determinate, indeterminate, or determinate/indeterminate).
troughcolor	sets the colour of the progress bar's trough.
background	sets the background colour.
relief	sets the relief style of the progress bar.
borderwidth	sets the width of the progress bar's border.
takefocus	specifies whether the progress bar can be included in the focus order.
disabledforeground	sets the foreground color of the progress bar when it is disabled.
activebackground	sets the background color of the progress bar when it is active.
activeforeground	sets the foreground color of the progress bar when it is active.
padx	sets the horizontal padding of the progress bar.
pady	sets the vertical padding of the progress bar.
text	sets the text to be displayed on the progress bar.
textvariable	specifies a Tkinter variable to hold the text displayed on the progress bar.

Example:

```
from tkinter import *
from tkinter import ttk

root = tk.Tk()
root.geometry("300x200")

def scale_changed(val):
    font_size = int(val)
    label.config(font=("TkDefaultFont", font_size))
```

```
    progress.config(value=font_size)

progress = ttk.Progressbar(root, orient="horizontal", length=200,
mode="determinate", value=1, maximum=48)
progress.pack()

scale = tk.Scale(root, from_=1, to=48, orient="horizontal",
command=scale_changed)
scale.pack()

label = tk.Label(root, text="Hello, World!", font=("TkDefaultFont", 10))
label.pack()

root.mainloop()
```

Output:

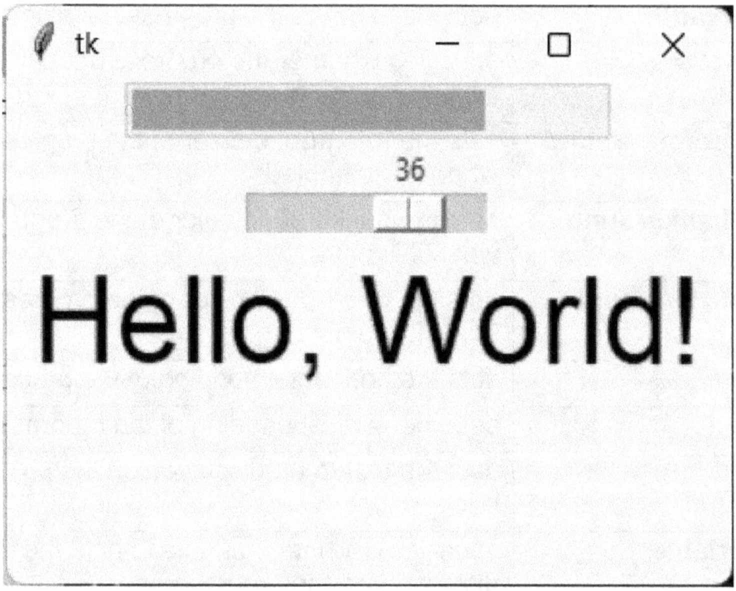

It is possible to use the Progressbar for lots of other things other than Progress. An example might be to show stock levels or the value of some sensor input.

Here we can see that the Progressbar shows not “progress” but the size of the font used for the “Hello, World!” Label as a percentage of the maximum set in the code.

Radiobutton

The Radiobutton widget allows the user to select one option from a group of available options. It is typically used in situations where the user needs to make a mutually exclusive choice from a set of options.

Syntax:

my_radio_button = Radiobutton(parent, options)

Options:

activebackground	sets the background color when the widget is active.
activeforeground	sets the foreground color when the widget is active.
bg or background	sets the background colour
bd or borderwidth	sets the width of the widget's border.
command	specifies a function that will be called when the button is selected.
cursor	sets the cursor to be displayed when the mouse is over the widget.
disabledforeground	sets the foreground color when the widget is disabled.
font	the font used to display text .
fg or foreground	sets the foreground color of the widget.
height	sets the height of the widget.
highlightbackground	sets the color of the widget's highlight when it does not have focus.
highlightcolor	sets the color of the widget's highlight when it has focus.
highlightthickness	sets the width of the widget's highlight.
image	specifies an image to be displayed.
justify	alignment of the text on the widget.
padx	sets the padding on the left and right sides of the widget.
pady	sets the padding on the top and bottom sides of the widget.
relief	sets the type of border to be displayed around the widget.
selectcolor	sets the color to be displayed when the widget is selected.

selectimage	specifies an image to be displayed when the widget is selected.
state	sets the state of the widget (normal, active, or disabled).
text	sets the text to be displayed on the widget.
textvariable	specifies a Tkinter variable to hold the text displayed on the widget.
underline	sets the index of the character that should be underlined in the text.
value	specifies the value to be associated with the widget when it is selected.
variable	specifies a Tkinter variable to hold the value associated with the widget when it is selected.
width	sets the width of the widget.

Example:

```
import tkinter as tk
root = tk.Tk()
# Define a Tkinter variable to store the selected RadioButton value
selected_option = tk.StringVar()

# Create the RadioButton widgets
option1 = tk.Radiobutton(root, text="Soup", variable=selected_option, value="Soup")
option2 = tk.Radiobutton(root, text="Beans", variable=selected_option, value="Beans")
option3 = tk.Radiobutton(root, text="Sandwich", variable=selected_option, value="Sandwich")
option4 = tk.Radiobutton(root, text="Potato", variable=selected_option, value="Potato")

# Pack the RadioButton widgets
option1.pack(padx=5, pady=5)
option2.pack(padx=5, pady=5)
option3.pack(padx=5, pady=5)
option4.pack(padx=5, pady=5)
root.mainloop()
```

Output:

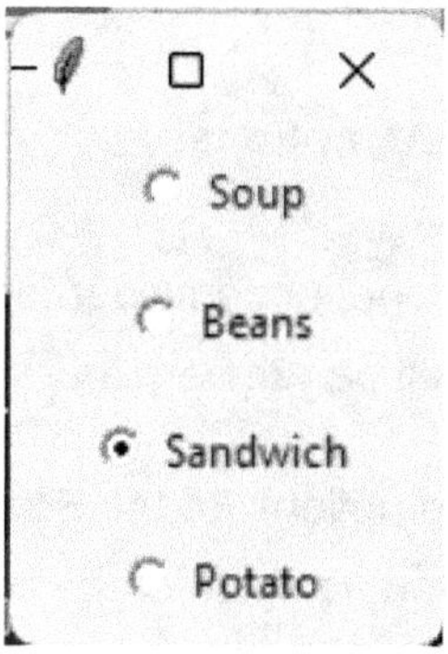

Scale

The scale widget allows users to select a value within a range by dragging a slider.

Syntax:

scale_widget = tk.Scale(parent, options)

where:

- **parent** is the parent widget or container for the Scale widget
- **options** are the optional parameters and configuration settings for the Scale widget

Here are some commonly used options for the Scale widget:

- **from_**: specifies the starting value of the scale (note the underline)
- **to**: specifies the ending value of the scale
- **orient**: specifies the orientation of the scale (either "horizontal" or "vertical")
- **length**: specifies the length of the scale
- **label**: specifies the label to display next to the scale
- **resolution**: specifies the precision of the values on the scale
- **command**: specifies the function to call whenever the scale value changes

Example

```
import tkinter as tk

def adjust_font_size(val):
    font_size = int(val)
    label.config(font=("TkDefaultFont", font_size))

root = tk.Tk()
root.geometry("200x200")

scale = tk.Scale(root, from_=10, to=36, orient="horizontal",
command=adjust_font_size)
scale.pack()

label = tk.Label(root, text="Hello, World!", font=("TkDefaultFont", 10))
label.pack()

root.mainloop()
```

Output:

Scrollbar

The Scrollbar widget is used to add a scrollbar to a widget that can be scrolled, such as a Text*or Canvas widget. The Scrollbar widget provides a way for the user to scroll the widget's contents up and down (or left and right, depending on the orientation of the scrollbar).

The Text widget can be very large (dependent on system memory) so the scrollbar is often vital if the amount of text displayed on the screen is far less than the amount of text.

Syntax:

scrollbar = tkinter.Scrollbar(parent, options)

Options include:

- **orient** Specifies the orientation of the scrollbar. Can be tk.HORIZONTAL or tk.VERTICAL.
- **command** Specifies a callback function to be called when the scrollbar is scrolled. The callback function should take one argument, which will be a floating-point value between 0.0 and 1.0 representing the position of the scrollbar.
- **bg** Specifies the background colour of the scrollbar.
- **fg** Specifies the foreground (text) colour of the scrollbar.
- **activebackground** Specifies the background colour of the scrollbar when it is in the active state.
- **troughcolor** Specifies the colour of the trough (background) of the scrollbar.
- **highlightcolor** Specifies the colour of the highlight rectangle, which is drawn around the scrollbar when it has the input focus.
- **width** Specifies the width of the scrollbar, in pixels.

Example adding a scrollbar to a Text widget:

```
import tkinter as tk

root = tk.Tk()
root.geometry("200x150")
root.title("Text Widget with Scrollbar")

# Create a scrollbar to the RIGHT
scrollbar = tk.Scrollbar(root)
scrollbar.pack(side=tk.RIGHT, fill=tk.Y)

# Create a text widget and attach the scrollbar to it
text_widget = tk.Text(root, yscrollcommand=scrollbar.set)
text_widget.pack(side=tk.LEFT, fill=tk.BOTH)
scrollbar.config(command=text_widget.yview)

# Insert some sample text into the text widget
text_widget.insert(tk.END, "Lorem ipsum dolor sit amet, consectetur adipiscing elit, sed do eiusmod tempor incididunt ut labore et dolore magna aliqua. Ut enim ad minim veniam, quis nostrud exercitation ullamco laboris nisi ut aliquip ex ea commodo consequat. Duis aute irure dolor in reprehenderit in voluptate velit esse cillum dolore eu fugiat nulla pariatur. Excepteur sint occaecat cupidatat non proident, sunt in culpa qui officia deserunt mollit anim id est laborum.")

root.mainloop()
```

Output

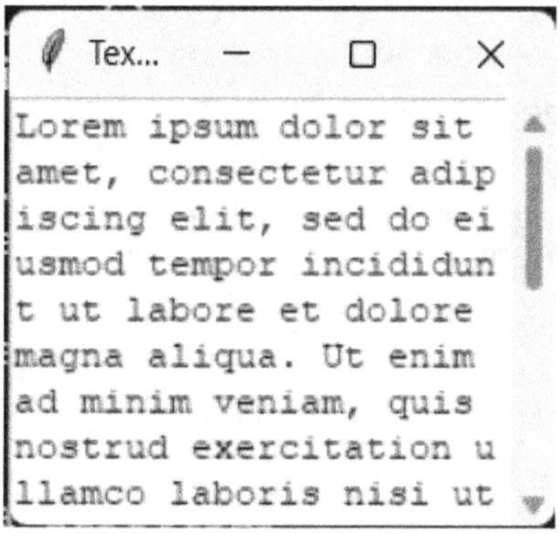

Scrollbar (ttk)

There is also a ttk version of the scrollbar widget which can use styles and themes. The **ttk.Scrollbar()** widget has a more modern appearance than the regular **Scrollbar()** widget.

ttk.Scrollbar Style options. Each option controls a different aspect of the scrollbar's appearance and behaviour. You can set these options using the style.configure() method:

Style Option	Description
arrowcolor	The colour of the scrollbar arrow.
arrowpadding	padding to apply to the scrollbar arrow.
arrowshape	The shape of the scrollbar arrow. The default value is **tkinter.ARROW**.
autoscrolllength	The length of the autoscroll region at the top and bottom of the scrollbar. The default is 0.
background	The background colour of the scrollbar.
bordercolor	The colour of the scrollbar border.
borderwidth	The width of the scrollbar border.
gripcount	The number of grip elements in the scrollbar. A grip is a small rectangle that the user can click and drag to scroll. The default value is 0, which means no grips are shown.
griplength	The length of each grip element.
grippadding	padding to apply to each grip element.
griprelief	The relief style of each grip element. The default value is **tkinter.RAISED**.
gripshape	The shape of each grip element. The default value is **tkinter.RECTANGLE**.
gripvisible	Whether or not to show the grip elements. The default value is **False**.
jump	The amount of content to jump when the user clicks on the scrollbar track (i.e., the area between the thumb and the arrows). The default value is 0, which means that the thumb jumps to the clicked position.
repeatdelay	The amount of time to wait before repeating the scroll action when the user holds down the scrollbar arrows or track. The default value is 0, which means that no repeat delay is used.
repeatinterval	The amount of time to wait between repeated scroll actions when the user holds down the scrollbar

	arrows or track. The default value is 0, which means that no repeat interval is used.
takefocus	Whether or not the scrollbar can receive focus. The default value is **False**.
troughcolor	The colour of the scrollbar trough (i.e., the area between the arrows and the thumb).
troughrelief	The relief style of the scrollbar trough. The default value is **tkinter.FLAT**. (SUNKEN, RAISED, GROOVED(
width	The width of the scrollbar.

Example:

```
import tkinter as tk
from tkinter import ttk

root = tk.Tk()
root.geometry("300x150")
root.title("Text Widget with ttk Scrollbar")

style = ttk.Style()
style.theme_use('default')

style.configure ("my_scrollbar.Vertical.TScrollbar", arrowcolor="blue",
troughcolor="red", width=25)

# Create a ttk scrollbar on the RIGHT
scrollbar = ttk.Scrollbar(root, style="my_scrollbar.Vertical.TScrollbar")
scrollbar.pack(side=tk.RIGHT, fill=tk.Y)
# Create a text widget and attach the scrollbar to it
text_widget = tk.Text(root, yscrollcommand=scrollbar.set)
text_widget.pack(side=tk.LEFT, fill=tk.BOTH)
scrollbar.config(command=text_widget.yview)

# Insert some text into the text widget
text_widget.insert(tk.END, "Lorem ipsum dolor sit amet, consectetur
adipiscing elit, sed do eiusmod tempor incididunt ut labore et dolore
magna aliqua. Ut enim ad minim veniam, quis nostrud exercitation
ullamco laboris nisi ut aliquip ex ea commodo consequat. Duis aute irure
```

```
dolor in reprehenderit in voluptate velit esse cillum dolore eu fugiat nulla
pariatur. Excepteur sint occaecat cupidatat non proident, sunt in culpa
qui officia deserunt mollit anim id est laborum.")


root.mainloop()
```

Output:

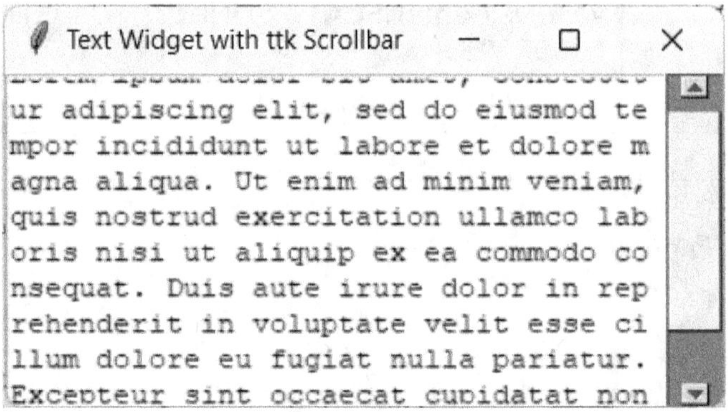

This is a slightly wacky example of a scrollbar just to show some of the options. The colours won't show in all editions on the book but the arrows are blue and the 'trough' is red.

Separator (ttk)

Separator is a widget used to create a visual separator between different widgets. It is often used to visually divide a window into sections or groups, or to visually separate different parts of the user interface.

The Separator widget is usually displayed as a horizontal or vertical line, which can be customized in terms of its width, height, and colour. It does not respond to events and is purely for visual purposes.

Syntax:

This is one of the widgets that is only available in Themed Tkinter ttk

separator_widget = ttk.Separator(parent, options)

Options

Option	Description
orient	sets the orientation of the separator. The value can be either "horizontal" or "vertical".
style	sets the style of the separator. By default, the separator uses the "TSeparator" style, but you can define your own custom style using the ttk.Style class.
padding	sets the amount of padding to be added around the separator. The value can be either a single integer, in which case the padding will be the same on all sides, or a tuple of four integers specifying the padding for each side in the order (left, top, right, bottom).

Example

```
import tkinter as tk
import tkinter.ttk as ttk

root = Tk()
root.title("Separators")
root.geometry("350x100")

label = Label(text="Above Separator")
label.pack()
# Create a horizontal separator
separator = ttk.Separator(root, orient='horizontal')
separator.pack(fill='x')
label = Label(text="Below Separator")
```

```
label.pack()

root.mainloop()
```

Output:

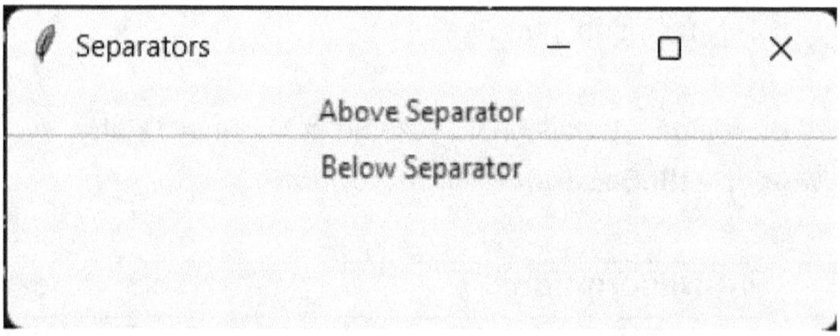

Sizegrip (ttk)

The ttk.Sizegrip widget is a small triangular widget that is used to provide a visual indication for resizing a window or frame. Sizegrip is part of the ttk (Themed Tkinter) module, which provides an updated and modernized set of widgets for Tkinter.

The ttk.Sizegrip widget is usually placed in the lower-right corner of a window or frame, and is designed to be used in conjunction with the tkinter.Grid geometry manager. When the user hovers the mouse over the ttk.Sizegrip, the cursor changes to indicate that the window or frame can be resized.

Syntax:

my_sizegrip = ttk.Sizegrip(parent, options)

Option	Description
style	The name of the style to use for the widget. This can be used to customize the appearance of the widget.
cursor	The cursor to use when the mouse is over the widget. This can be used to change the cursor to a different icon to indicate that the user can resize the window or frame.
takefocus	Whether the widget should be included in the focus traversal order. By default, this is set to False, which means that the widget will not receive keyboard focus when the user presses the Tab key.
width	The width of the widget in pixels. By default, this is set to 10.
height	The height of the widget in pixels. By default, this is set to 10.

Example (interesting as it uses both pack and gris geometry methods):

```
import tkinter as tk
from tkinter import ttk

root = tk.Tk()
root.geometry("300x100")
root.title("Sizegrip")

# Create a frame with a label and a sizegrip widget
my_frame = ttk.Frame(root)
my_label = ttk.Label(my_frame, text="Resizable frame")
my_sizegrip = ttk.Sizegrip(my_frame)

# Pack the label and sizegrip widgets inside the frame
my_label.pack(side="left", padx=5, pady=5)
my_sizegrip.pack(side="right", padx=5, pady=5, anchor="se")

# Use the grid geometry manager to resize the frame
my_frame.grid(column=0, row=0, sticky="nsew")

# Configure the grid to resize with the window
root.columnconfigure(0, weight=1)
root.rowconfigure(0, weight=1)

root.mainloop()
```

Output:

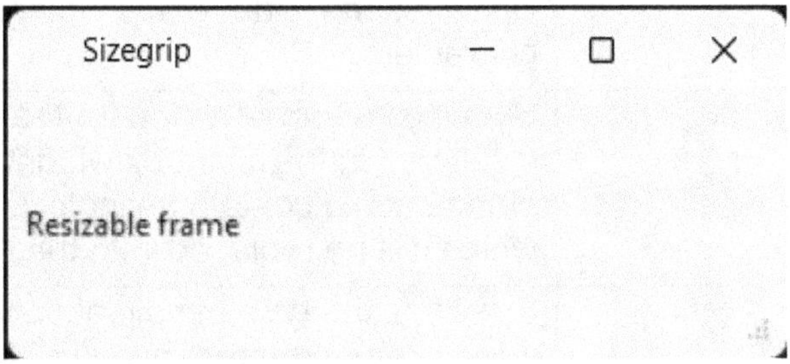

Note the Sizegrip in the lower right corner.

Spinbox

Spinbox is a widget that allows the user to select a value from a fixed set of options by changing the value using up and down arrow buttons or the mouse scroll wheel. The Spinbox widget can be used to provide a user interface for selecting a numerical value or a value from a list.

Syntax:

my_spinbox = Spinbox(parent, options)

Options:

Option	Description
from_	Specifies the lower limit of the range of values that can be selected. Use from_ (with an underscore) instead of from as from is a reserved keyword.
to	Specifies the upper limit of the range of values that can be selected.
increment or increment	Specifies the amount by which the value should be incremented or decremented when the up or down arrow buttons are clicked.
values	Specifies a list of values to choose from.
textvariable	Specifies a tkinter.StringVar object that will be used to set and get the current value of the Spinbox widget as a string.
state	Specifies the state of the Spinbox widget. Valid values are "normal", "readonly", and "disabled".
wrap	Specifies whether the value should wrap around from the highest value to the lowest value and vice versa. Set to True to enable wrapping, False to disable it.
width	Specifies the width of the Spinbox widget in characters.
format	Specifies a format string for the value displayed in the Spinbox widget. The format string should contain a single %s placeholder, which will be replaced with the current value.
validate	Specifies the type of validation to perform when the user enters a value in the Spinbox widget. Valid values are "key", "focus", "all", and "none".
validatecommand	Specifies a callback function to validate the

	current value of the Spinbox widget. The function should return True if the value is valid, otherwise False..

Example:

```
import tkinter as tk

root = tk.Tk()
root.geometry("300x100")
root.title("Spinbox")

# Create a Spinbox with a range of values
spinbox1 = tk.Spinbox(root, from_=0, to=10, increment=2, font="Arial 16")
spinbox1.pack()

# Create a Spinbox with a list of values
spinbox2 = tk.Spinbox(root, values=("Red", "Green", "Blue"),
font="Helvetica 16")
spinbox2.pack()

# Create a Spinbox with a StringVar and a custom format
value = tk.StringVar()
value.set("1")
spinbox3 = tk.Spinbox(root, from_=0, to=10, textvariable=value,
format="%03.1f", font="Arial 16")
spinbox3.pack()

root.mainloop()
```

Output:

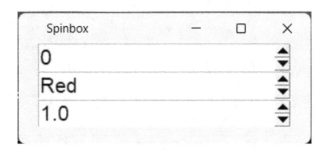

Text

The Text widget is one of the most powerful standard widgets provided by the Python tkinter module as it can be used both to input text and to display text. It is a popular choice for building text editors, word processors, and other text-related applications.

Features of the Text widget:

The Text widget allows the user to edit text using a keyboard or mouse. It provides features like copy and paste, undo and redo, and text selection.

- **Formatting** The Text widget supports text formatting, including font styles (such as bold and italic), colours, and alignment.
- **Tags** The Text widget allows you to apply "tags" to regions of text, which can be used to control the formatting or behaviour of the text. For example, you could apply a tag to all occurrences of a particular word to highlight or manipulate them in some way.
- **Scrolling** The Text widget supports scrolling of text that exceeds the widget's visible area. The user can scroll using the mouse wheel or scrollbar, or programmatically using the widget's scroll methods.
- **Input and output** The Text widget can be used for both input and output of text. You can read the contents of the widget using its get() method, and write text to the widget using its insert() method.

Syntax:

text_widget = tk.Text(parent, options)

where **parent** is the parent widget and **options** is a list of configuration options for the widget.

Options:

Option	Description
bg	The background color of the widget.
fg	The text color of the widget.
font	The font used for the text in the widget.
height	The number of lines displayed in the widget.
width	The number of characters that can be displayed on a line.
padx	The padding to the left and right of the widget.
pady	The padding above and below the widget.
wrap	The way the text wraps when it reaches the edge of the widget. The options are NONE, CHAR, WORD, or ALL.
state	Whether the widget is disabled or not. The options are NORMAL or DISABLED.
insertbackground	The color of the cursor.

highlightcolor	The color of the text highlight when it is selected.
highlightthickness	The thickness of the text highlight when it is selected.
selectbackground	The color of the background when text is selected.
selectforeground	The color of the text when it is selected.

Example:

```
import tkinter as tk

root = tk.Tk()
root.geometry('300x200')
root.title("Text Widget Example")

# Create a Text widget and add it to the GUI
text_widget = tk.Text(root, height=6, width=35)
text_widget.pack()
# Add a label to the GUI
label = tk.Label(root, text="Enter text:")
label.pack()

# Define a function to retrieve the contents of the Text widget
def get_text():
    text = text_widget.get('1.0', 'end-1c') # retrieve text without trailing newline
character
    print(f"You entered: {text}")

# Add a button to the GUI that calls the get_text() function when clicked
button = tk.Button(root, text="Submit", command=get_text)
button.pack()

root.mainloop()
```

Output:

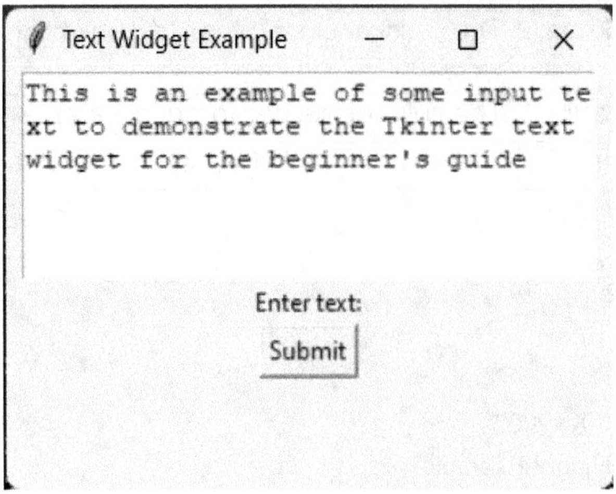
Text Widget Example
This is an example of some input te
xt to demonstrate the Tkinter text
widget for the beginner's guide
Enter text:
Submit

Getting Text from the Text widget

If like me, you find the Entry widget a bit limiting, you can use the Text widget as an alternative data entry field particularly if you want to be able to enter multiple lines of text.

text_widget.get(start, end)

is a method of a Text widget that retrieves the text content of the widget within a specified range.

Here are some common ways to specify the **start** and **end** arguments:

- **start** and **end** are both None: This will return all the text content of the Text widget.
- **start** is a tuple (line, column) and end is None: This will return the text content of the line specified by line.
- **start** is a tuple (line, column) and **end** is also a tuple (line, column): This will return the text content between the two specified positions.
- **start** and **end** are both strings representing a position in the Text widget: These strings must be in the format line.column, where line is the line number and column is the character offset within the line. For example, "**1.0**" represents the first character of the first line in the Text widget.

Once you have specified the range of text that you want to retrieve, the **get()** method will return a string containing the text within that range.

Example:

text_content = text_widget.get('1.0', 'end-1c')

This example will retrieve the text from the Text widget from the first character of the first line until the end. Note that using "end-1c" instead of just "end" is useful when don't want to include the final newline character in the retrieved text.

Treeview (ttk)

The Treeview widget is a part of the ttk module in tkinter. The Treeview widget provides a way to display and manipulate hierarchical data in a tabular format.

Syntax:

tree = ttk.Treeview(parent, columns=("column1", "column2", ...), options)

Here, parent is root (e.g., a Tk or Toplevel instance) and options is a list of configuration options for the widget.

The columns argument specifies the column names for the Treeview widget, starting with the special column "#0" for the tree hierarchy. The remaining columns are identified by name, and each corresponds to a single value in the data hierarchy.

The **insert()** method is used to add items to the Treeview widget. The first argument is the ID of the parent item, or an empty string "" to insert at the top level. The second argument is where to insert the item: "end" for the end of the list, or an existing item ID to insert before that item. The text argument specifies the label for the item, and the values argument is a tuple of values to be displayed in the columns corresponding to the column names.

The **heading()** method is used to set the headings for each column, starting with "#0" for the tree hierarchy column. The text argument specifies the text to display in the heading.

Options

- **columns** specifies the column names of the treeview
- **displaycolumns** specifies the columns to display
- **height** specifies the number of rows to display
- **selectmode** specifies the selection mode (e.g., 'browse', 'extended', 'none')
- **show** specifies what elements to show (e.g., 'headings', 'tree')
- **style** specifies the style to use
- **takefocus** specifies whether the treeview can receive focus
- **xscrollcommand** and **yscrollcommand**: specify scrollbars for the treeview
- **padding** specifies the padding for the treeview
- **selectforeground** and **selectbackground**: specify the foreground and background colours for selected items
- **font** specifies the font for the text in the treeview
- **separator** specifies the separator character for column values

Methods:

- **treeview_name.column(column_name, option, value=None)** sets or retrieves options for a specific column
- **treeview_name.insert(parent, index, iid=None, **kw)** inserts a new item into the treeview
    - **parent** here is not root or the name of the window but the ID of the parent item, or an empty string if the item has no parent.
    - **iid** The ID to use for the new item. If None is provided (the default), a unique ID will be generated automatically.
- **treeview_name.delete(*items)** deletes one or more items from the treeview
- **treeview_name.detach(*items)** detaches one or more items from the treeview
- **treeview_name.move(item, parent, index)** moves an item to a new location in the treeview
- **treeview_name.selection()** retrieves the currently selected items
- **treeview_name.focus(item=None)** sets or retrieves the item that has focus
- **treeview_name.see(item)** ensures that an item is visible in the treeview
- **treeview_name.set(item, column, value) sets** the value of a specific column for an item
- **treeview_name.item(item=None, option=None, **kw)** sets or retrieves options for an item or the treeview as a whole
- **treeview_name.tag_configure(tag_name, **options)** configures a tag to apply a certain style to items with that tag
- **treeview_name.bind(sequence, function, add=None)** binds a function to an event for the treeview or its items

NB: **kw = Any number of keyword arguments can be provided, where the key is the name of a column and the value is the value to display in that column for the new item.

Example:

```
import tkinter as tk
from tkinter import ttk

# create the tkinter GUI window
root = tk.Tk()
root.title("Treeview Example")

# create the Treeview widget
tree = ttk.Treeview(root, columns=("name", "age"))

# set column headings
tree.heading("#0", text="ID")
tree.heading("name", text="Name")
tree.heading("age", text="Age")

# add some data
tree.insert("", "end", "001", text="001", values=("Alice", 25))
tree.insert("", "end", "002", text="002", values=("Bob", 35))
tree.insert("", "end", "003", text="003", values=("Charlie", 45))

# create sub-items
subitem = tree.insert("001", "end", "001a", text="001a", values=("Sub-
name 1", 55))
subitem = tree.insert("001a", "end", "001b", text="001b", values=("Sub-
name 2", 65))
subitem = tree.insert("003", "end", "003a", text="003a", values=("Sub-
name 3", 67))

# pack the Treeview widget into the GUI
tree.pack()
```

```
# run the main tkinter event loop
root.mainloop()
```

Output:

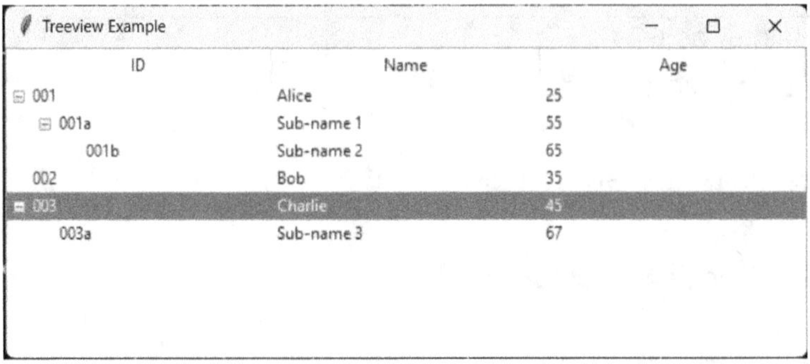

Time and Date

I'm often writing code to report on events between certain times and dates and need an interface to allow the user to select date and time ranges. I nearly wrote something like this from scratch and then realised that I would be reinventing the wheel.

To add a graphical time and date selector in Python Tkinter, you can use the **tkcalendar** module. This module provides a **Calendar** widget that can be used to select a date, and a **TimeEntry** widget that can be used to select a time.

If you haven't already done so, you may find that you need to install **tkcalendar** with

pip install tkcalendar

Please note that the **TimeEntry** option was only introduced in **tkcalendar** version **1.6** so if you already have it, please check your version and update it if needed:

import tkcalendar

print(tkcalendar.__version__)

I use tkcalendar primarily for the **DateEntry** and **TimeEntry** widgets which allow the user to enter a date and/or time value through a graphical user interface. **Tkcalendar** also provides some other features:

- Display calendars in different sizes and orientations
- Customise the look and feel of the calendar, including background colour, font, and colours for both selected and disabled dates
- The ability to restrict the range of selectable dates to a specific range or exclude certain dates
- Support for different languages and date formats
- Conversion between different time zones.

DateEntry widget

Syntax:

my_date = DateEntry(parent, options)

DateEntry Example. You will note that being based in the UK, I have used the **date_pattern** option to specify a British date format.

Common options (see the tkcalendar documentation for the full list):

Option	Description
date_pattern	This option sets the format of the date displayed in the widget. The default format is "yyyy-mm-dd", but you can set it to any valid date format string.
mindate	This option sets the minimum date that can be selected in the widget. The value should be a datetime.date object.
maxdate	This option sets the maximum date that can be selected in the widget. The value should be a datetime.date object.
locale	This option sets the locale used to display the date in the widget. The value should be a string specifying the locale, such as "en_US".
firstweekday	This option sets the first day of the week. The value should be an integer representing the weekday, where 0 is Monday.
showweeknumbers	This option specifies whether to show the week numbers in the widget. The value should be a boolean (True or False).
selectmode	This option sets the selection mode of the widget. The value can be "day", "week", "month", or "year", depending on what level of granularity you want to allow the user to select.
year	This option sets the initial year displayed in the widget. The value should be an integer.
month	This option sets the initial month displayed in the widget. The value is an integer between 1 and 12.
day	This option sets the initial day displayed in the widget. The value should be an integer between 1 and 31, depending on the selected month.
selectbackground	This option sets the background colour of the selected date.

selectforeground	This option sets the text colour of the selected date.
normalbackground	This option sets the background colour of the unselected dates.
normalforeground	This option sets the text colour of the unselected dates.
weekendbackground	This option sets the background colour of the weekends.
weekendforeground	This option sets the text colour of the weekends.

Example:

```
from tkcalendar import DateEntry
import tkinter as tk
root = tk.Tk()
root.geometry("200x50")

date_entry = DateEntry(root, width=10, background='blue',
foreground='white', borderwidth=4, date_pattern='dd/mm/yyyy',
font="Helvetica 14")
date_entry.pack(padx=10, pady=10)

root.mainloop()
```

Output (surrounded by my Windows background)

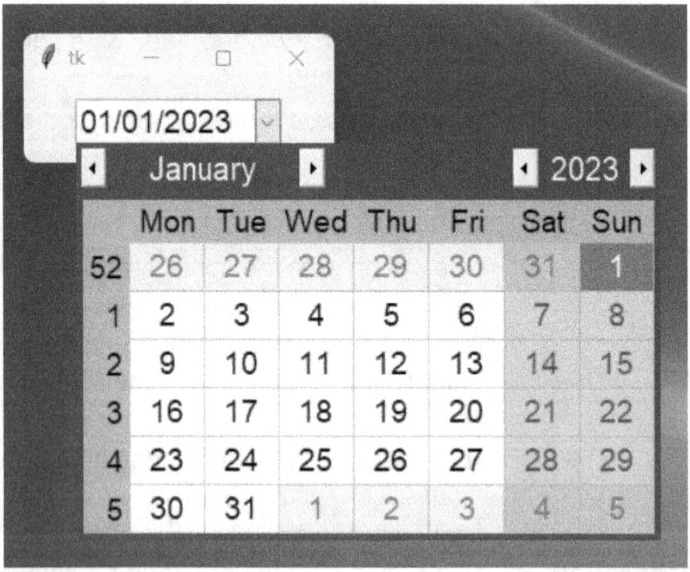

TimeEntry widget

NB: You will need tkcalendar version 1.6 or greater for TimeEntry

Syntax

my_time = TimeEntry(root, options)

Common options (see the tkcalendar documentation for the full list)

Option	Description
font	This option sets the font used to display the time. The value should be a tuple that specifies the font family, size, and style.
foreground	This option sets the colour of the text in the widget.
background	This option sets the background colour of the widget.
width	This option sets the width of the widget.
format	This option sets the format of the time displayed in the widget. The default format is "HH:MM:ss"
textvariable	This option sets a tkinter variable that will be updated with the selected time. The value should be a tkinter.StringVar or tkinter.IntVar.
validate	This option sets the validation mode for the widget. The value should be "key" or "focus". If set to "key", the widget will validate each keystroke as it is entered. If set to "focus", the widget will validate the entire time when it loses focus.
validatecommand	This option sets a callback function that will be called to validate the input in the widget. The function should return True if the input is valid, or False if it is not.
increment	This option sets the increment for the time values. The default value is 1 minute, but you can set it to any number of minutes or seconds.
am_pm	This option specifies whether to use 12-hour or 24-hour format for the time. The value should be a boolean (True for 12-hour format, False for 24-hour format).
timeformat	This option sets the format for the time values in the drop-down list. The default value is

	"HH:MM"
foreground_highlight	This option sets the colour of the selected time.
background_highlight	This option sets the background colour of the selected time.

Example:

```
# ensure you have tkcalendar 1.6 or later
from tkcalendar import TimeEntry
import tkinter as tk

root = tk.Tk()

# Create a TimeEntry widget
my_time = TimeEntry(root, width=12, background='blue',
foreground='white', foreground_highlight='red')

my_time.pack() # Pack the widget

root.mainloop() # Start the main event loop
```

Running Python in Windows without the Console

Once you have tested and debugged your Python code, you may well want to create desktop icons that invoke the GUI applications without opening a console window. The key to this is using the **pyw** file extension rather than **py**.

Files with a "**.pyw**" extension are Python scripts that run in the background without displaying a console window.

When you double-click on a .pyw file, the file is executed by the Python interpreter without displaying a console window. On Windows, the file extension is associated with the Python interpreter by default, so as long as Python is installed on your system, the **.pyw** files should be executed correctly.

.**pyw** files can behave slightly different from regular **.py** files, especially when it comes to handling errors and exceptions. By default, any unhandled exceptions in a .**pyw** script will be silently ignored, which can make debugging more difficult. To avoid this, you can use the logging module or ensure that the code is debugged before moving to **.pyw**.

The End

www.ingramcontent.com/pod-product-compliance
Lightning Source LLC
La Vergne TN
LVHW051746050326
832903LV00029B/2743